1939-1945
WORLD WAR TWO

AUTHOR

Paolo Crippa (23 April 1978) has cultivated his passion for Italian history since high school. His research interests are focused mainly in the field of military history and in particular on italian armored units from the 30s until the end of World War II. In 2006 he published his first volume, *"I Reparti Corazzati della Repubblica Sociale Italiana 1943/1945"*, the first organic research carried out and published in Italy on the subject. In 2007 he published *"Duecento Volti della R.S.I."* and in 2011 *" Un anno con il 27° Reggimento Artiglieria Legnano"*. He regularly contributes to several journals: Milites, New Historica, SGM - World War II, Batailes & Blindes, Armoured Vehicles and history of the twentieth century, Mezzi Corazzati, both as an author, or in collaboration with other researchers. He published with the editor Mattioli 1885 in 2014 *"Italy 43 – 45 – Civil War improvised AFV's"* (2014), *"Italian AFV's of the Civil War 1943 - 1945"* (2015) and *"Italy 43 – 45 – AFV's and MV's of co-belligerent units"* (2018).

Titolo: **ITALIAN TANKERS IN THE DODECANESE 1940-1945** Code.: **WTW-032 EN** Di Paolo Crippa

ISBN code: 978-88-93278317 prima edizione Marzo 2022

Text: English Nr. of images: 124 Layout: 177,8x254mm Cover & Art Design: Luca S. Cristini

WITNESS TO WAR (SOLDIERSHOP) is a trademark of Luca Cristini Editore, via Orio, 35/4 - 24050 Zanica (BG) ITALY.

WITNESS TO WAR

ITALIAN TANKERS IN THE DODECANESE 1940 - 1945

PHOTOS & IMAGES FROM WORLD WARTIME ARCHIVES

PAOLO CRIPPA

BOOKS TO COLLECT

INDICE

L3/35 3a Compagnia - Operazione "Merkur"

PREFACE

I loved the islands of the Dodecanese at first sight, when I landed there for the first time back in 2006. I learned about Rhodes and its history, both the most distant and the most recent, history that speaks the Italian language, I became passionate and deepened the military events that characterized the archipelago during the years of Fascism.

Thus I discovered that in this remote corner of the Mediterranean sea in the 40s of the last century a small unit of Italian tank crews was sent, the CCCXII Mixed Tank Battalion of the Aegean, an unknown and forgotten unit, of which very little official documentation exists. Despite not having taken part in war clashes, due to the isolation to which the Italian Aegean Islands were condemned, if not the invasion of Crete in 1941, this department was touched by pain and death after the Armistice, when the almost all the tankmen were taken prisoner by the Germans and many of them tragically died in the sinking of the steamers that carried them from the Aegean to Europe, a huge tragedy unjustly forgotten.

Acknowledgments

First of all, I would like to thank Antonio Fragassi, veteran of the CCCXII Tank Battalion, who granted me an interview years ago, sharing his memories and also making available the photographs taken during his stay in Rhodes. I also thank his nephew Alessandro for the great availability he has shown me over the years, whenever I need to contact him for clarification. I also thank Francesco Pedonesi, who kindly made available the photographs of his father Dante, tanker of the CCCXII, and wanted to share his memories. My thanks also to Pasquale Iengo, nephew of the same name of a tank driver of the Battalion, and Alberto Durgante, nephew of Lieutenant Augusto Durgante, both soldiers perished in the sinking of the "Oria" steamship.

Finally, I thank my friend Antonio Tallillo for his collaboration in iconographic research.

Paolo Crippa

▲ Landing company of the Royal Navy arriving in the Aegean in 1912.

▲ The port of Rhodes seen from a seaplane in flight in the summer of 1941 (ACS).

▼ Seaplanes in the port of Rhodes in 1942: the connection between the islands of the Dodecanese and between the archipelago and Italy was held by seaplane lines (ACS).

▲ Works at the base of the MAS on the island of Lero in the winter of 1942 (ACS).

▼ An armed ship transports troops of the Royal Army and Blackshirts to the island of Samos in the summer of 1941 (ACS).

▲ A Carabiniere on board the steamship "Fiume", a ship that performed scheduled service between the Aegean islands (ACS).

THE ITALIAN DODECANESE

The Dodecanese, a group of islands in the Southern Sporades, represented an important supply base for the Turkish garrisons during the Libyan War. For this reason, in February 1912, Admiral Thaon di Ravel had planned its occupation; on the following 26 April the island of Stampalia was occupied and on 4 May the Italian Expeditionary Force landed in Rhodes, which was completely occupied on the 17th.

In retaliation, the Turkish government expelled about 70,000 Italians from the Ottoman Empire, although many managed to stay because they were employed in European companies located there.

By virtue of the Peace Treaty of Lausanne of 18 October 1912, the Italian presence in the Dodecanese was to be limited to the time necessary for the eviction of the Turks from Tripolitania and Cyrenaica, but given the ambiguity of the treaty and the protracted "resistance" in Libya, England and France (London Pact of April 26, 1915) recognized Italy as having full rights over the islands, confirming their dominion by a clause of the Treaty of Sèvres (August 10, 1920) and by the subsequent Peace of Lausanne of July 24, 1923.

The Italian military administration of the Dodecanese lasted until 7 August 1920, when the first civil governorship was established. Initially, it was decided to identify the Dodecanese not as a colony but as a possession (we were faced with a "white" population and did not want to upset the local irredentist movement, which proved to be largely in favor of the Italian occupation). The government of the estate was based in Rhodes, in the islands it was represented by a regent and the local populations were represented by the Council of Mayors, with only consultative powers on some administrative aspects.

In 1925 the resident population before the Treaty of Lausanne obtained Italian citizenship, although without political rights and without the obligation of military service.

In 1930, the archipelago was elevated to the rank of colony with the name of the Italian Aegean Islands; 1936 marked the beginning of a period of fascism for the archipelago, with the arrival of Cesare Maria De Vecchi, count of Val Cismon, after a long period of prosperity.

At the outbreak of the Second World War, the Dodecanese suddenly found itself isolated from the motherland. Its defenses had been strengthened by virtue of a progressive militarization of the islands (there were a total of about 50,000 soldiers, but with scarce armaments and means, including the Army, Navy and Air Force), there were three military airports (in Rhodes those of Maritza and of Gadurrà) and naval bases (remember those of the MAS of Rodie and, above all, that of Lero). The island of Rhodes was garrisoned by the "Regina" Infantry Division, on which the CCXIII Aegean Mixed Tank Battalion operationally depended. The presence of a considerable British fleet, however, made the navigation of the Italian merchant fleet dangerous. Governor De Vecchi was first replaced by General Ettore Bastico in 1941, who was himself replaced by Admiral Inigo Campioni in 1942.

Far from the motherland, the archipelago was relegated to a secondary role during the conflict, but the population suffered hunger for long periods, due to the difficulty of supplying food, since the islands were not fully self-sufficient. The Armistice led to a worsening of conditions, due to the German occupation, which also resulted in the deportation of the local Jewish community.

On 9 May 1945, the landing of the English troops on the islands was completed, putting an end to Italian sovereignty over the archipelago; the signing of the Paris Peace Treaty on 10 February 1947 and the handing over of the islands to Greece marked the definitive end of Italian rule.

"Regina" Infantry Division

The 50th "Regina" Infantry Division was derived from the "Regina" Brigade of the Sardinian Army and, after complex organic events, in 1938 the Murge Brigade ceded the 9th and 10th "Regina" Infantry Regiment to the Regio Army of the Islands Troops Command islands of the Aegean[1]. On 1 March 1939 the Royal Army Troops Command of the Italian Aegean Islands was raised to the level of the Infantry Division, with the 9th and 10th "Regina" Infantry Regiment and the 50th Divisional Artillery Regiment in staff. In 1940 the 201st Aegean Militia Legion "Conte Verde" and the CCCXII Tank Battalion were also assigned to the division.

The Division served as a permanent garrison for the whole of the Italian Dodecanese, with headquarters in Rhodes and main detachments on the islands of Lero, Kos, Scarpanto, Caso, Calino, Castelrosso, Stampalia, Patmo and Gaidaro. The Artillery Regiment was located in Rhodes, with the main positions located on Mount Fileremo, and among the tasks of the Division there was also the garrison of the Gadurrà and Marizza airports.

The large unit was marginally involved in the war events of the Second World War. On November 20, 1940, two Companies of the 1st Battalion of the 10th Regiment took control of the islet of Gaidaro, occupied in the previous days by Greek sailors, while in March 1941 the 4th Battalion of the same Regiment reoccupied Castelrosso, where an English unit had landed.

During the Greek Campaign units of the 10th Regiment, supported by German units, occupied the islands of Amorgos, Anafi, Io, Santorini, Naxos, Paros, Andro, Tino, Termia, Zea, Serfanto, Sira, Mikonos, Samo, Icaria and other smaller islands. At the end of the same month, the 1st Battalion of the 9th Regiment and the 2nd Battalion of the 10th Regiment participated in the "Merkur" Operation, forming the backbone of the "Caffaro" Tactical Group, together with the 50th Company of 47/32 and the 3rd Tank Company of the CCCXII Mixed Tank Battalion.

The Division remained and continued the activity of territorial garrison and coastal defense of the Dodecanese islands until the tragic events of September 1943.

At the outbreak of the Second World War, the Division presented the following order of battle:

- Divisional Infantry Command
- 9th "Regina" Infantry Regiment
- 10th "Regina" Infantry Regiment
- 201st Aegean Legion "Green Count"
- L Mortar Battalion
- 50th "Regina" Artillery Regiment
- 91st Company of Genius artists
- 46th Compagnia Genio telegraphers and radiotelegraphers
- 50th Chemical Company
- Divisional services
- Army Corps Troops
  - "Aegean" Regi Carabinieri Group
  - "Dodecanese" coverage area
  - CCXII Mixed Tank Battalion
  - 35th Artillery Grouping from a coastal position
  - LVI Autonomous Anti-aircraft Artillery Group
  - Autonomous group Artillery from coastal position "Coo"
  - Autonomous group Artillery from coastal position "Scarpanto"
  - Army Corps Service

---

[1] The 9th "Regina" was stationed in the Italian Dodecanese since 1924 and the Regimental Command coincided with the Troops Command.

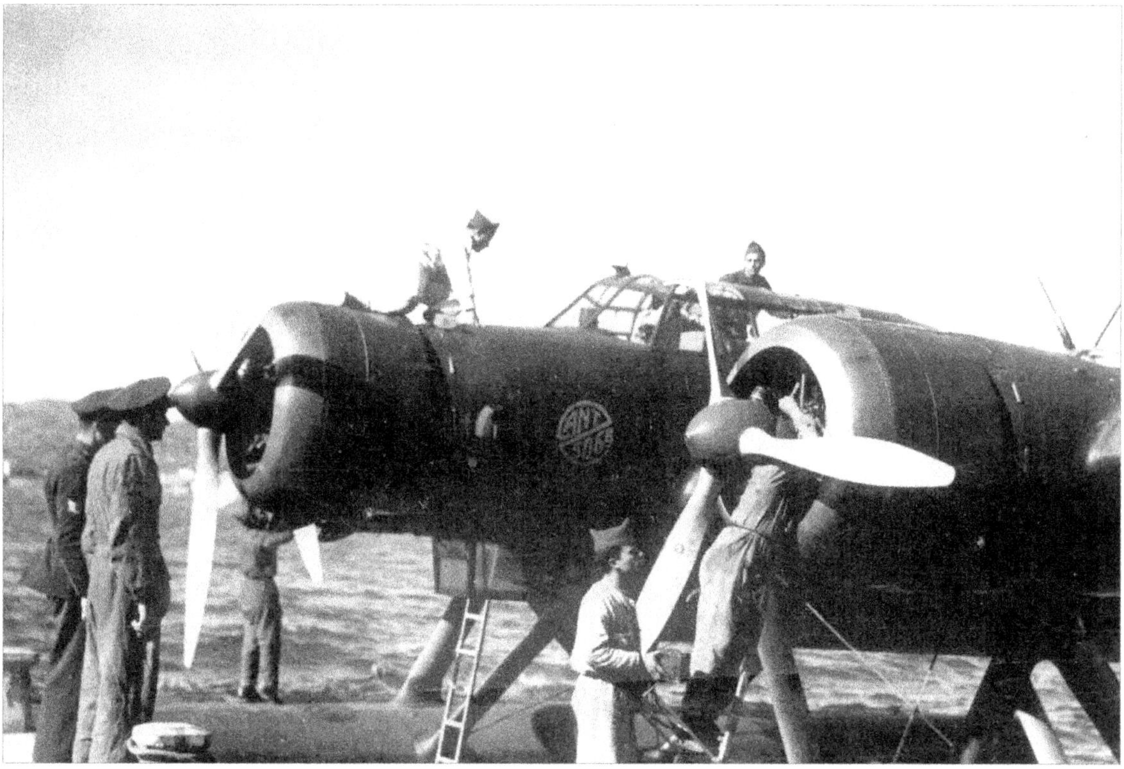

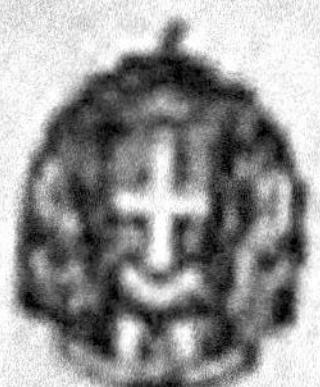

▲ Preparations for the departure of seaplanes from the island of Lero for a reconnaissance mission in the winter of 1942 (ACS).

▼ Letterhead of the Armed Forces Command of the Italian Aegean Islands (EGEOMIL).

COMANDO FORZE ARMATE
DELLE ISOLE ITALIANE DELL'EGEO

IL COLONNELLO CAPO DI S. M.

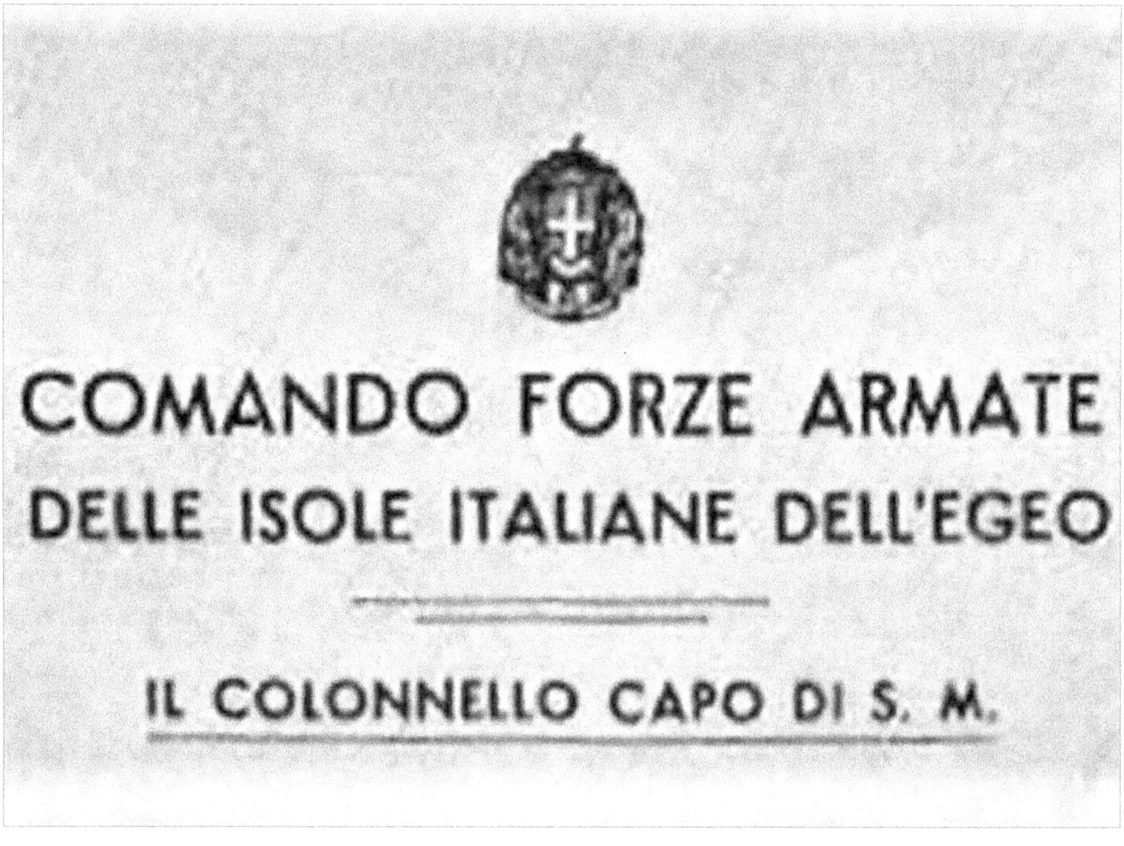

▲ A group of infantrymen of the "Queen" Division: the large unit was destined to garrison Rhodes, with detachments in the smaller islands.

▼ A MAS sailing in the waters off the island of Rhodes in the winter of 1942. Two important MAS bases were present in Rhodes and Leros (ACS).

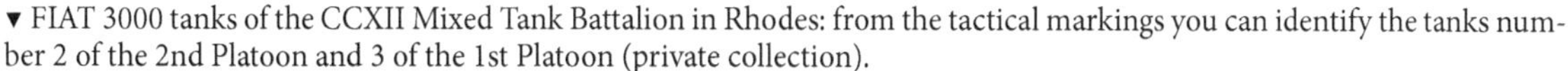

▲ A group of Italian soldiers observing above the walls of the old city of Rhodes, winter of 1942 (ACS).

▼ FIAT 3000 tanks of the CCXII Mixed Tank Battalion in Rhodes: from the tactical markings you can identify the tanks number 2 of the 2nd Platoon and 3 of the 1st Platoon (private collection).

▲ Letter sent by a corporal of the tank crew from Rhodes: note both the handwritten military post address and the Battalion stamp, indicated as "CCCXII Tank Battalion" (private collection).

▼ L3 light tanks that have just arrived in the Dodecanese: they should be vehicles belonging to the Company of Captain Fabio Fabi (private collection).

▲ Group photo of Tankers of the CCXII Battalion around a light tank in Rhodes (private collection).

▼ Even on the island of Rhodes, the tankmen continued to be constantly subjected to physical exercises of various kinds: in this photo the overcoming of a wall, carried out with the bandolier, which was carried on board armored vehicles (private collection).

▲ Tank crews of the CCCXII: the soldier on the left wears the gray-green regulatory uniform, while the one on the left wears a one-piece blue suit (private collection).

▲ A FIAT 3000 tank of the 1st Company is transported aboard a chariot cart on a dusty road on the island of Rhodes, during a joint exercise with infantry units (private collection).

▼ In a photograph taken on the same occasion as the previous one, it can be seen that the trolley was towed by a Lance RO truck; on the turret of the tank you can see the tactical markings (probably tank number 1 of the 1st Platoon). On the far left of the image, among the bush, we can see the turret of a second FIAT 3000, also probably self-transported (private collection).

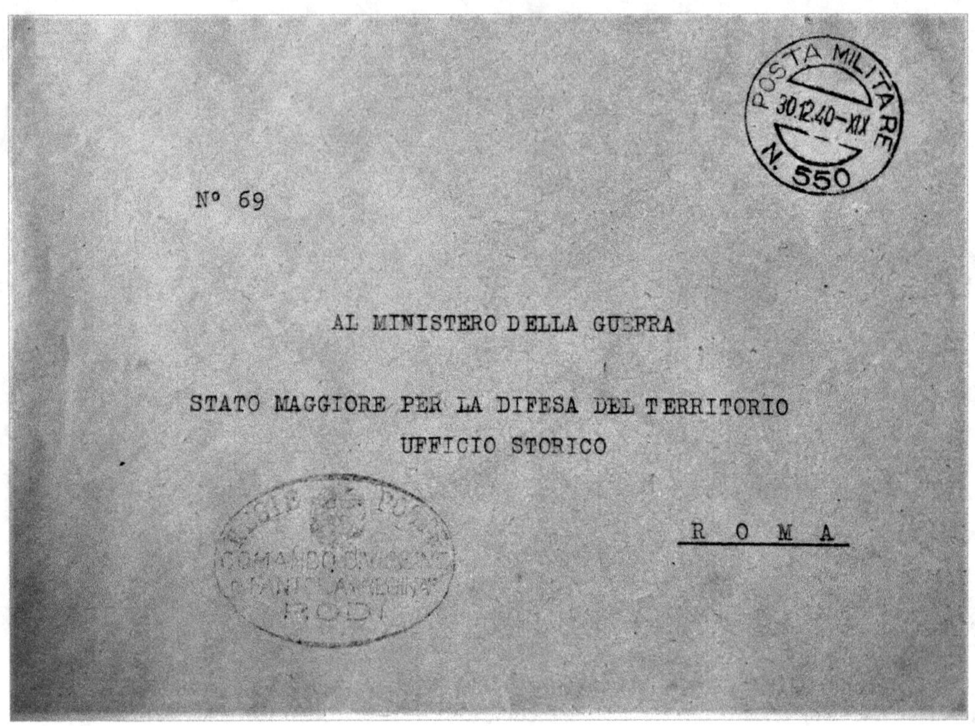

▲ Letter sent from the Command of the "Regina" Division to the Ministry of War: the Military Post stamp shows the Military Post number 550, common to all the departments located in the Aegean (private collection).

▼ Interesting document dated December 1941 from the Mixed Aegean Troop Depot of Barletta, on which the CCCXII Aegean Tank Battalion depended (private collection).

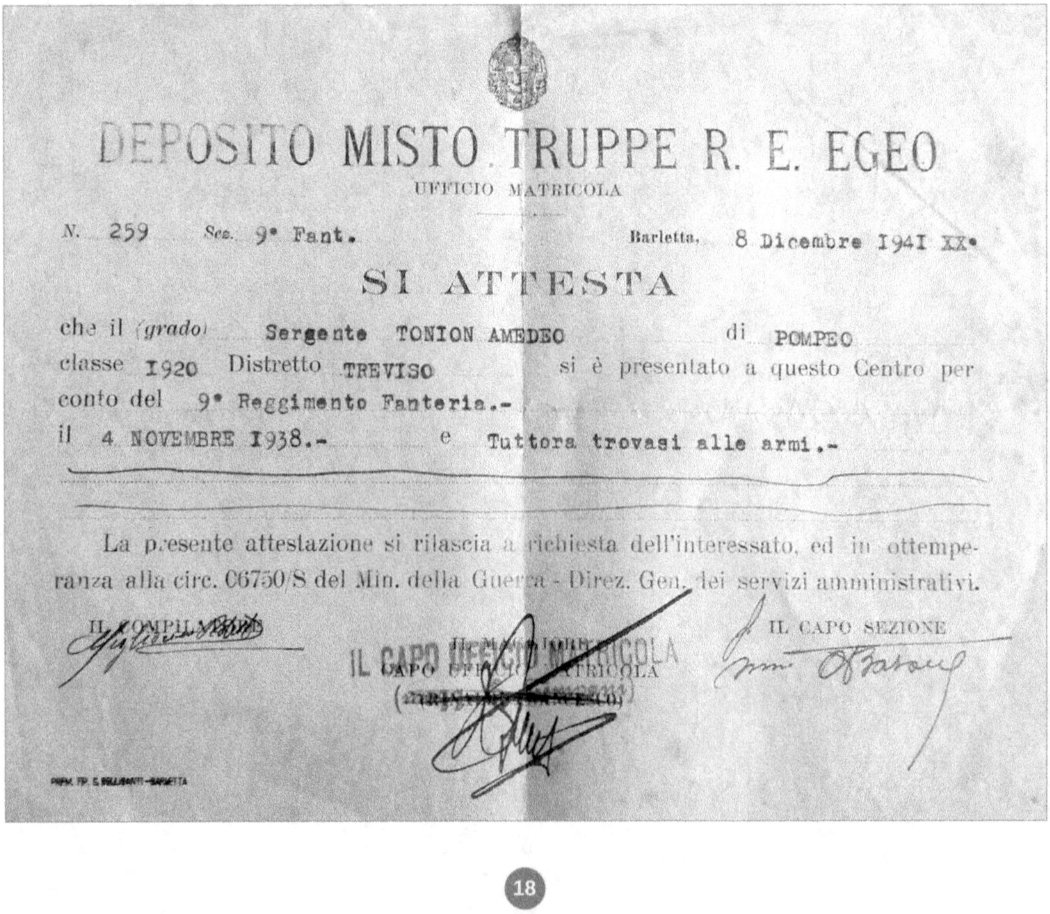

DEPOSITO MISTO TRUPPE R. E. EGEO

UFFICIO MATRICOLA

N. 259   Sez. 9° Fant.   Barletta, 8 Dicembre 1941 XX°

SI ATTESTA

che il (grado)   Sergente TONION AMEDEO   di POMPEO
classe 1920 Distretto TREVISO   si è presentato a questo Centro per
conto del 9° Reggimento Fanteria.-
il 4 NOVEMBRE 1938.-   e   Tuttora trovasi alle armi.-

La presente attestazione si rilascia a richiesta dell'interessato, ed in ottemperanza alla circ. C6750/S del Min. della Guerra - Direz. Gen. dei servizi amministrativi.

IL COMPILATORE   IL CAPO UFFICIO MATRICOLA   IL CAPO SEZIONE
                          (   )

▲ Tanker of the CCCXII aboard a truck, probably a Dovunque 35 (private collection).

▲ In the days before the Italian mission to Crete, a landing exercise was held in Rhodes, which involved the departments assigned to the operation. In the photo, light tanks of the CCCXII Battalion disembark from the gangway mounted on the river ship "Porto di Roma", the only one suitable for transporting motor vehicles.

▼ Protected by some L3 tanks of the Mixed Aegean Battalion, infantrymen of the "Regina" Division landed during the landing tests in view of the operation on Crete: already on this occasion the preparation and the shipping appeared completely unsuitable for an operation amphibious.

▲ The motor vehicles are also disembarked from the "Port of Rome" ship during the exercise before the attack on Crete (Tallillo).

▲ Loading of the armored vehicles on the "Port of Rome" before leaving for Crete: the wagon in the photograph is number 4 of the 3rd Platoon of the 3rd Company (Benvenuti - Colonna).

▼ Italian soldiers board trucks to be transported to the embarkation area for Crete; among them some tankers of the CCCXII (ACS).

▲ Military personnel on break with a dog-mascot on duty at the Gadurrà airfield (Rhodes) in the summer of 1941 (Ufficio storico dell'esercito).

▼ Italian soldiers observe the sea from the walls of the city of Rhodes, winter 1942 (Ufficio storico dell'esercito).

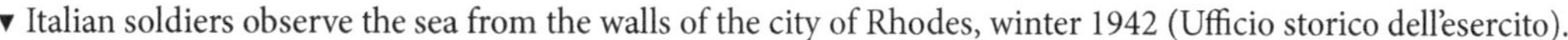

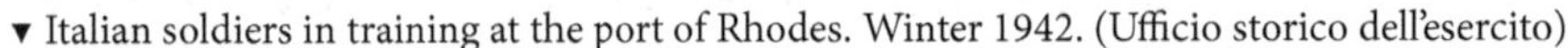

▲ Soldiers at the port of Rhodes in the summer of 1941 (Ufficio storico dell'esercito)

▼ Italian soldiers in training at the port of Rhodes. Winter 1942. (Ufficio storico dell'esercito)

CCCXIII BATTAGLIONE CARRI MISTO DELL'EGEO (CCCXIII MIXED TANK BATTALION OF THE AEGEAN)

THE FIRST ARMORED UNITS IN THE AEGEAN

As we have seen, in this corner of the Aegean, which might seem, at first glance, strategically of secondary importance, but which is actually a gateway to the Middle East, the high Italian Commands always maintained a decent military contingent. The control of the islands was entrusted to the 50th "Regina" Infantry Division, to flight and ground departments of the Regia Aeronautica and contingents of the Regia Marina, concentrated in the base of the island of Lero. With the rather sudden evolution of the tanker specialty, following the Great War, it was almost inevitable to send armored vehicles to the Dodecanese, also in consideration of the importance that the archipelago could play in the context of a possible international conflict that could also interest the countries of the eastern Mediterranean, then British and French colonies.

The first armored vehicles to arrive in the Aegean were most likely old armored cars Ansaldo Lancia 1ZM of the Royal Carabinieri. In fact, in 1926 the Arma dei Carabinieri received 34 Lancia 1ZMs armed with FIAT 14 machine guns, which were framed in an armored car battalion, soon dissolved; the armored cars remained in charge, however, to the Carabinieri and 2 of them were sent to Rhodes, employed by the Regi Carabinieri Group of the Aegean.

A Company of the Royal Carabinieri Machine Gun Cyclists was established on the island in 1936, which incorporated the 2 Lancias; this Company was organized on:

- Platoon Machine Gunners Cyclists (with 3 small cars armed with Saint Etienne machine guns and 2 motorcycles armed with machine guns)
- Platoon Cyclists (with 50 cyclists and 2 motorcyclists Carabinieri)
- Lancia 1ZM section (with the 2 armored cars).

The Company had been strongly desired by the Governor of the De Vecchi archipelago, but its operational utility was undoubtedly scarce. In the meantime, on an unspecified date, a Platoon consisting of 4 Lancia 1ZM armored cars with crews from the Royal Army had been sent to Rhodes.

The Special Tank Company for the Aegean

With the evolution of the international situation, it seemed evident that the presence of only old-built armored cars was no longer sufficient to guarantee effective support of armored vehicles to the garrison troops in the archipelago (the Lancia 1ZM dates back to the Great War). For this reason, in the first half of 1939 a "Special Tank Company for the Aegean" was set up within the 3rd Armored Infantry Regiment, with 12 L3 tanks of different versions. The Company, under the command of Captain Fabio Fabi, was almost immediately transferred to the dependencies of the 4th Tank Infantry Regiment (May 20, 1939), to subsequently move definitively to the Mixed Troops Depot of the Aegean[2].

In Rhodes, the Company was thus incorporated into the CCCXII Mixed Tank Battalion of the Aegean, also formed by the few armored units already present on the island, namely the Platoon of

---

2 The Royal Aegean Army Mixed Depot was located in Barletta, near the barracks in via Andria, and had been set up specifically to supply men, equipment and armaments to the troops of the Royal Dodecanese Army. Therefore, all the departments mobilized in the Aegean depended on it, including the CCCXII Mixed Tank Battalion and the units assigned to it, such as the Special Tank Company for the Aegean.

4 armored cars of the Army and the Lancia Section of the Royal Carabinieri; the Special Tank Company for the Aegean became in all likelihood the 3rd Company of the CCCXII Battalion.

The 3rd Frontier Tank Company

In March 1940 the 3rd Frontier Tank Company was established in Caserta[3], under the command of Lieutenant Pasquale Mele and dependent on the G.a.F., Guardia alla Frontiera, with 2 platoons of FIAT 3000B tanks and a mixed platoon of M21 and M30. The Company was destined for the Italian islands of the Aegean and, at the time of its transfer to the Dodecanese (on a date that could not be identified in 1940, probably in late spring), this department should have represented the maneuvering mass of the departments tankers of the archipelago.

The Company had this war staff, established with the order of February 6, 1940:
- Command Platoon (with a 37/40 cannon-armed command tank)
  - Command team
  - Repair and recovery team 1st Platoon (L5 model 30 tanks)
- 2nd Platoon (L5 model 30 tanks)
- 3rd Mixed Platoon (L5 model 21 and model 30 tanks)

The Command Platoon had a staff of 4 officers, 3 non-commissioned officers and 25 tankers and had a car, two motorcycles and a trailer. Other vehicles possibly necessary for the operation of the platoon, i.e. 5 light trucks or two heavy trucks, one of which with a trailer, were made available from time to time by the 50th Aegean Mixed Autobahn, on the orders of the Command of the Armed Forces of the island of Rhodes.

In July 1942, Lieutenant Giovanni Furetti took over from Lieutenant Pasquale Mele at the helm of the Compagnia Carri L5.

THE FORMATION OF THE CCXXII MIXED TANK BATTALION

The CCCXII Mixed Tank Battalion drew its origins directly from the II Breaking Tank Battalion of the 2nd Tank Regiment. In 1938 the Battalion changed its name to CCCXII Tank Battalion L "Suarez", absorbed by the 31st Tank Infantry Regiment.

On May 20, 1939, the Battalion became dependent on the 4th Tank Infantry Regiment of Rome, to subsequently move definitively to the mobilization load of the Mixed Aegean Troops Depot on March 30, 1940. The Battalion was sent to Rhodes on March 30, 1940, probably equipped with only L wagons, no more than a dozen) and was located in Psito, in the center of the island (initially with the address of Military Post No. 505R, i.e. Rhodes, later changed to 505E, for Aegean, in fear that it could be easily detected by British espionage), employed by the "Regina" Infantry Division.

---

3 The Guardia alla Frontiera also had 5 companies of tanks among its staff, formed between December 1939 and the beginning of 1940, all equipped with the old Fiat 3000 Model 21 and 30. The objective they wanted to pursue with the establishment of these unit was precisely to structure departments that could use the still efficient FIAT 3000 tanks, assigning them to permanent Army Corps (and it is for this reason that one of these companies was destined to the Dodecanese, a theater considered absolutely static and intended only to be defended). At the time of the entry into the war, the 2nd, 4th and 5th Companies were located close to the French border: the material was already obsolete from the start and this did not allow it to be profitable during the Comrade of France. The end of the conflict with Yugoslavia led to the dissolution of these three companies and the storage of tanks in the depots of the original tank units, tanks which were then reused in the airport defense of Sicily, being destroyed during the Allied landing in July - August 1943. The 1st Company was deployed in Albana and, after the end of hostilities with Greece, it passed to the dependence of the Troop Command of Montenegro and was harshly used to counter the guerrilla actions of the partisans, while the 3rd was destined, as we have seen at Aegean. Over time, the Fiat 3000 wagons, both due to their seniority and the lack of spare parts, ended up largely abandoned in the warehouses of the G.a.F. belonging or underground to use them as small defensive works.

In September, with the completion of the transfer to the Aegean of the Company of Captain Fabi [4], the CCXXII Mixed Tank Battalion (its final name), under the command of Lieutenant Colonel Amedeo d'Agello, assumed this organic form:

- Command Company
    - o Armored Car Scouting Platoon (with 6 Lancia 1ZM and a motorcycle)
- 1st Company L5 tanks (with 10/12 FIAT 3000) under the command of Lieutenant Mele
- 2nd Company L3 wagons (with 8 L3 wagons)
- 3rd Company L3 wagons (with 8 L3 wagons) under the command of captain Fabio Fabi [5]

The 1st L5 Tank Company, which was none other than the 3rd Frontier Tank Company, was initially called Compagnia Carri M, as the FIAT3000 tanks were considered medium tanks, until the M11/39 tanks entered the line.

According to some sources, the Battalion also depended on 2 autonomous Platoons of L3 wagons, the first with 4 and the second with 3 wagons, located in the smaller islands of the archipelago.

During the Second World War, the tank personnel assigned to the Battalion, while passing through the Mixed Aegean Depot of Barletta, came exclusively from the 4th Tank Regiment of Rome. Many tankmen, even after their arrival in Rhodes, continued to wear the number 4 in the round bar of the headgear frieze, indicating the Regiment of origin.

After Italy entered the war, the armored vehicles present in the Dodecanese were never involved in any war action, but, on the other hand, the entire archipelago was only marginally affected by the war events. The only military operation in which they were called to participate was the occupation of the island of Crete (operation "Merkur"), planned and implemented by the German commands without the Italians being informed. The decision to invade the island, in fact, was taken by Hitler as early as April 1941, without involving the allies.

"MERKUR" OPERATION

The decision to occupy Crete, at the end of the Greek Campaign (somewhat disastrous for Italy), was taken exclusively by the German Commands, without consulting the Italian counterparts, and Hitler himself personally ordered to proceed with the attack on the 25th. April 1941 [6]. The attack plan was based exclusively on an air operation and envisaged the 7th Fleegerdivision occupying the three airports of the island, in order to subsequently bring in airborne ground departments, with a limited support of supplies by sea. [7]

---

4 Some publications erroneously indicate Captain Fabio Fabi as commander of the entire Battalion; in reality, the Battalion was initially commanded by Lieutenant Colonel Amedeo d'Ajello, who was replaced in 1942 by Lieutenant Colonel Iunio Masini. Fabi commanded the 3rd Company until the end of the conflict.

5 For the sake of completeness of information, we also report this organic structure indicated by some publications:
- Command
- 1st Company L5 tanks
- 2nd Company L5 tanks
- 3rd Company L3 tanks

However, it seems very unlikely that two wagon companies equipped with FIAT 3000 were drawn from the meager equipment of the 3rd Frontier Tank Company.

Another organization chart found online indicates this structure:
- 1st CV33 wagon company
- 2nd Company L5 / 30 tanks.

6 The possession of Crete, in addition to concluding the Greek Campaign, as we have seen in the text, sheltered the oil wells of Ploesti in Romania, vital for the support of the Germanic armed forces, especially in view of the invasion of Russia. In fact, there was the risk that Allied bombers departing from Crete could have carried out missions on the Romanian extraction wells, putting the supplies for the Germans in crisis..

7 Occupation carried out by air was a very risky but obligatory choice. The massive presence of the Royal Navy, in fact, made it almost impossible to launch an amphibious attack on the island.

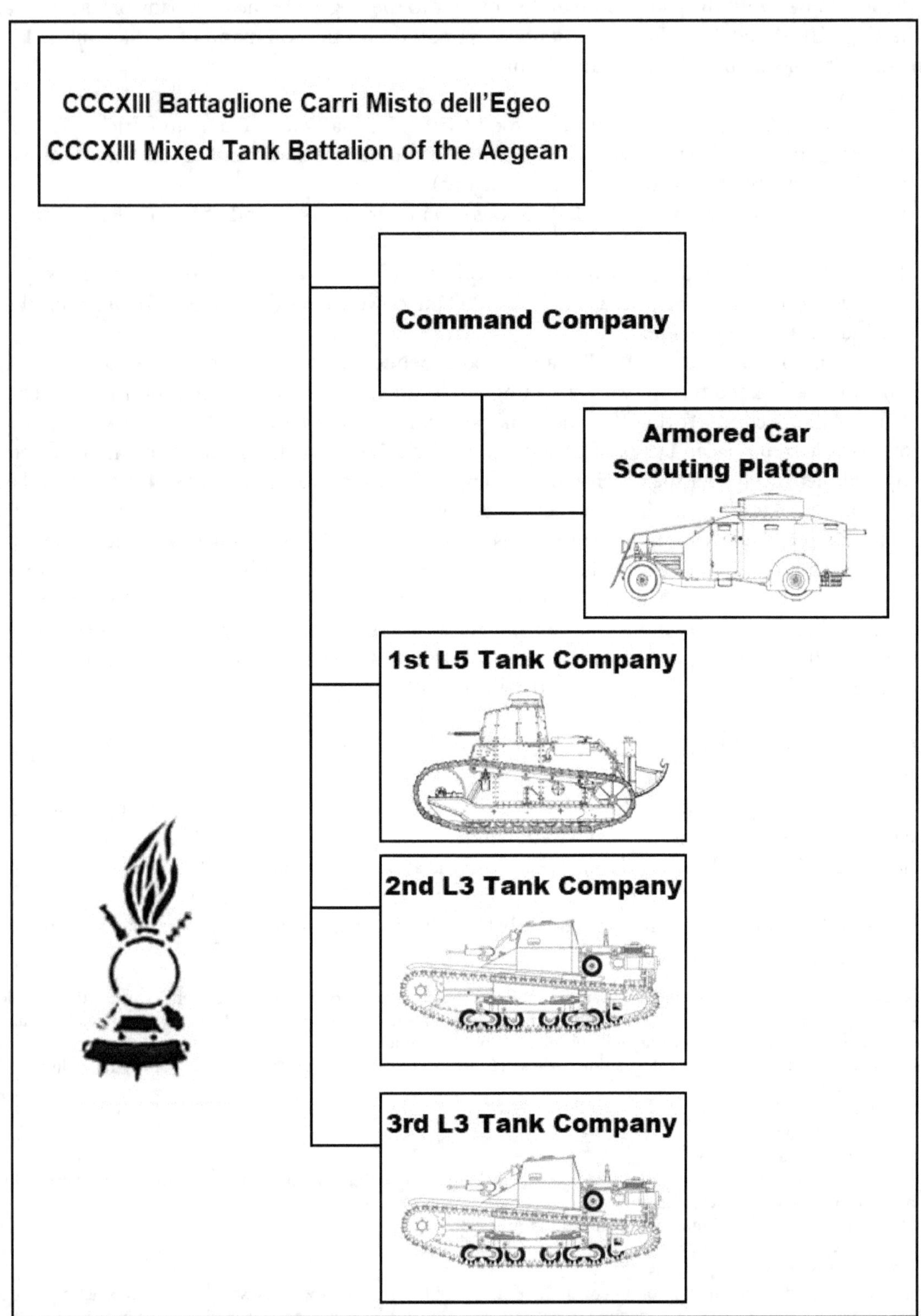

▲ Organization chart of a light tank battalion in the Dodecanese (Author's diagram)

The Italian commands in the Aegean, left in the dark, were only asked to concentrate their torpedo boats in the port of Piraeus, without providing further explanations. The German attack was launched on May 20, 1941 and the beginning was not the most favorable for the German forces. The launch of the German paratroopers, who also employed 63 gliders, was split into two brackets due to a lack of aircraft and the attack took a bad turn for the Fallschirmjäger right from the start; only in Maleme, in the western part of the island, did the paratroopers manage to create a small bridgehead in the airport, which was used the next day to land the 5th Mountain Division, with an operation that however caused numerous deaths among the Germanic ranks. From this moment, however, the Germans began to gain ground and overwhelm the British and Greek troops stationed on the island.

Upon hearing of the German attack, the Italian Commands immediately asked to be able to take part in it and Mussolini himself gave the order to quickly organize a small Italian invasion force. However, the Italian proposals were effectively rejected by the Germans. On the same day of May 21, however, two German convoys, loaded with supplies, were intercepted by the British navy and had to return to Athens, after suffering heavy losses. It was therefore necessary for the German commands to accept an Italian intervention in the operation, to alleviate the pressure that had been created on the German units. During a meeting held on 22 May in Athens at the Command of the 4.Luftflotte, the captain Corso Pecori Giraldi (commander of MARISUDEST) was officially asked to give rise to a landing in the eastern part of the island to be carried out with troops and vehicles taken from the Dodecanese. After a series of exchanges of conflicting points of view between the Italian Commands, on the evening of 23 May the Governor Ettore Bastico received an order from General Cavallero to proceed with the planning of the expedition, which was to employ two reinforced infantry battalions and support services. , for a total of about 2,500 men. On 25 May Bastico communicated to the Supreme Command that the Italian expeditionary force would leave Rhodes at 18 on the 27th, to land on the afternoon of the 28th in the bay of Sitia, the easternmost of the northern coast of Crete, with the aim of advancing towards southwest to occupy Jerapetra, as requested by the Germans. On the same day, a landing exercise was conducted in Rhodes, with somewhat disappointing results and, although it was clear that it would be necessary to further train the troops involved in the landing in Rhodes, it was decided to proceed with the plan anyway. Given the dangerousness of the crossing, which, although short-lived could be threatened by the English ships that beat the Cretan waters, the unusual decision was taken to disembark in the early afternoon[8], so that the convoy was in Canale di Caso at a time when aerial reconnaissance could have guaranteed the "green light".

The command of the maritime expedition was entrusted to the vessel captain Aldo Cocchia, who found himself leading this gathering and heterogeneous flotilla, gathered in a hurry using what was possible to find in Rhodes.:

- 2 small coastal steamers: "Giorgio Orsini"[9] e "Tarquinia"
- 1 lagoon vaporetto: "Giampaolo"
- 2 tugs: "Aguglia" and "Impero"
- 1 river ship: "Port of Rome" (transformed into a tank landing ship),
- 2 refrigerated fishing motor vessels: "Assab" and "Addis Abeba"
- 4 fishing boats: "Sant'Antonio", "San Giorgio", "Pluto" and "Navigatore"
- 1 tanker: "Nera"
- 2 port cisterns: CG 89 and CG 167

Most of the shipping was unsuitable for transporting and, above all, for landing troops; the fishing boats had been equipped at the bow with landing gangways, completely useless because the too

---

8 To exploit the favor of darkness, amphibious operations are generally conducted at dawn.
9 It was chosen as the headquarters of the Command at sea.

high draft of the boats did not allow them to get close enough to the coast, so as to be able to lower the piers. The troops traveled in difficult conditions, forced to remain on deck, on ships without kitchens and toilets.[10]. Only the "Port of Rome", a river ship, moved to the Aegean with the function of minesweeper, was the only boat suitable for draft and load capacity suitable for an amphibious operation, since it was able to reach the shoreline and, thanks to a sturdy mobile wooden bridge mounted in the bow, it could land heavy material. For this reason the Company Carri L3, strong of 13 tanks, was embarked on this ship.

The escort to the convoy consisted of:
- 1 destroyer: "Crispi"
- 3 torpedo boats: "Libra", Lince" e "Lira"
- 6 MAS

The Italian Expeditionary Corps, commanded by Infantry Colonel Ettore Caffaro, was made up of about 2,500 men from the following units:
- I Infantry Battalion of the 9th Infantry Regiment of the "Regina" Division
- II Infantry Battalion of the 10th Infantry Regiment of the "Regina" Division
- 50th Company 47/32 anti-tank guns
- 3rd Company Carri L3 / 35 of the CCCXII Mixed Tank Battalion, commanded by captain Fabio Fabi
- 2 Companies of Sailors
- departments of Black Shirts
- departments of the Royal Carabinieri

The heavy armament consisted of 46 FIAT machine guns, 6 81 mm mortars, 18 45 mm mortars, 6 65/17 guns, 6 47/32 guns, 13 L3 tanks. Given the nature of the island and the state of the road network, the supply of motor vehicles was very limited (3 cars, 1 light truck and 9 motorcycles), but 205 mules were present to ensure the transport of the impediments.

The landing site had been chosen on May 26, during an aerial reconnaissance carried out by the captain of the vessel Cocchia.

The embarkation of the expeditionary force began at 11 on May 27 and lasted until 17, when the first boats began to set sail. In the early hours of the next day the convoy met the escort units. The navigation continued, albeit at a very low speed, almost calm, apart from the mistral wind and a deviation to make the route more direct, due to an alarm relating to the signaling of an approaching British formation. Around 4 pm the convoy reached Capo Sidero, a place destined for landing; the "Crispi" began to bomb the lighthouse and at 5pm the landing in the harbor of Sitia began, after the "Gaimpaolo" was moored to a small pier, while the "Orsini", the "Aguglia" and the "Port of Rome" had run aground on the beach. These are the first coins of the landing in the words of the captain Cocchia: "*In a couple of minutes, the tanks slide down from the "Port of Rome", across the appropriate bridge, and occupy the strongholds of the position. The sailors of the landing companies land, stand down, lay out flying pontoons, organize the ferries, set the boats in motion. The individual operations follow one another quickly and feverishly, but precise, so much so that at 5.20 pm all the three thousand men of the Expeditionary Corps are in Sitia[11]*".

---

10 It should be noted that the decision to use these means had been taken into consideration that large tonnage ships, in addition to being more vulnerable, would have had to stop off the coast and transship troops and materials onto the boats to carry out the landing. The chosen units were concentrated in Rhodes in forty-eight hours and each of them was assigned a naval officer as military commander.
11 Aldo Cocchia, "Aspetti Navali dello sbarco a Creta", book cited in the bibliography.

In the inhabited area of Sitia, cleared of civilians, the Italian departments met the resistance of about 200 Greek soldiers, who were soon overwhelmed, while the L3 tank platoons of the CCCXII were sent in advance to the west and the bulk of the Expeditionary Corps was grouped together. north-west of the country. The unloading operations lasted all night and the march was resumed the next day around noon, heading towards Jerapetra. The avant-garde encountered some outbreaks of resistance and in the evening tanks of the 3rd Company had reached Exo Mouliana.

On May 30, the Expeditionary Force resumed its march, headed for the set goal, the junction on the roadway to Jerapetra, in order to complete the mission within the day. Caffaro had given the order to continue, if necessary, even in the dark, until the goal was reached. The wagons of the CCCXII occupied the crossroads around 19.00, after having sustained a clash against the weak resistance opposed by Greek units. Major Ruta, who commanded the vanguard, sent a motorcyclist relay to the main part of the troop still on the march, which communicated that the Italian tanks had made contact with the 55th German Fusilier Battalion. On May 31, the bulk of the Expeditionary Corps reached Jerapetra, placing themselves at the disposal of General Ringel, commander of the 5th Gebirgsdivision which was completing control of the western part of the island of Crete.

At the end of the fighting, the 3rd Carri Company (or at least part of it) which had participated in the landing, remained in charge of the island of Crete. There are some uncertainties about the rate left in Crete. In fact, there is no certainty about the number of chariots left in Crete, but it can be assumed that they were probably at least 6, by virtue of the fact that this number of chariots was present on the island at the time of the 1943 Armistice, nor has it been possible to ascertain whether Captain Fabi remained in Crete in command of the Company or whether he returned to Rhodes[12].

The Expeditionary Corps was almost completely returned to Rhodes and temporarily replaced by a landing company of the Royal Navy. At the end of September 1941 the transfer of the 51st Infantry Division "Siena" from Greece to Crete began, where it carried out garrison and control tasks in the eastern part of the island, an area assigned to Italy. The 3rd Tank Company was consequently assigned to the Division and later assumed the name of 51st L Tank Company.

Captain Fabio Fabi, who had successfully commanded the Carri Company during the "Merkur" operation, was awarded the War Cross for Military Valor with the following motivation:

"Commander of an L tank company in a complex operational cycle, he led his department with skill and determined will. In numerous daring episodes he achieved the objectives indicated by eliminating the subsequent opposing resistances. Island of Crete, May 28 - June 4, 1941".

From a general point of view, for the Germans the conquest of Crete had a huge cost in terms of losses (about 50% of the paratroopers died or were wounded), while the Italian Expeditionary Corps achieved some success, considering the tremendous improvisation. with which the expedition was conducted, even if it is necessary to underline that, at the time of the arrival of the Italians, the island was now almost 90% occupied. The Italians then, given that the British contingent had by now been vanquished (captured or fled by sea), had to endure very limited clashes with only Greek units, reporting insignificant losses.

THE ARMISTICE AND IMPRISONMENT

After the occupation of Crete, life for the Italian military contingent in the Aegean (and also for the Mixed Tank Battalion) returned to being quiet and characterized only by the typical garrison activities.

---

12 In reality, it is not even clarified by any document whether the tanks of the 3rd Company remained in Crete at the end of Operation "Merkur" or if they were brought in at a later time, with the arrival on the island of the "Siena" Division in month of september.

In 1942 the command of the CCXII Battalion was entrusted to Lieutenant Colonel Iunio Masini and in July of the same year the Lieutenant Giovanni Furetti took over from Lieutenant Mele at the helm of the Compagnia Carri L5. Over time, many of the battalion's tanks, especially the oldest ones such as the FIAT 3000, became unusable due to non-repairable failures due to the lack of spare parts, thus gradually reducing the operational capacity of the department. However, mobility on the islands was always difficult: the already scarce fuel was very frequently sold illegally by some Italian officers to Greek civilians.

The organization of the CCCXII was consequently changed and, to overcome the shortage of armored vehicles, a Mixed Speedy Company was established with the crews left without wagons, under the command of Captain Pasquale Candida.

In any case, hordes of personnel continued to arrive from Italy, both officers, non-commissioned officers and troops, from the 4th Tank Regiment, passing through the Aegean Troops Depot in Barletta, practically up to the Armistice.

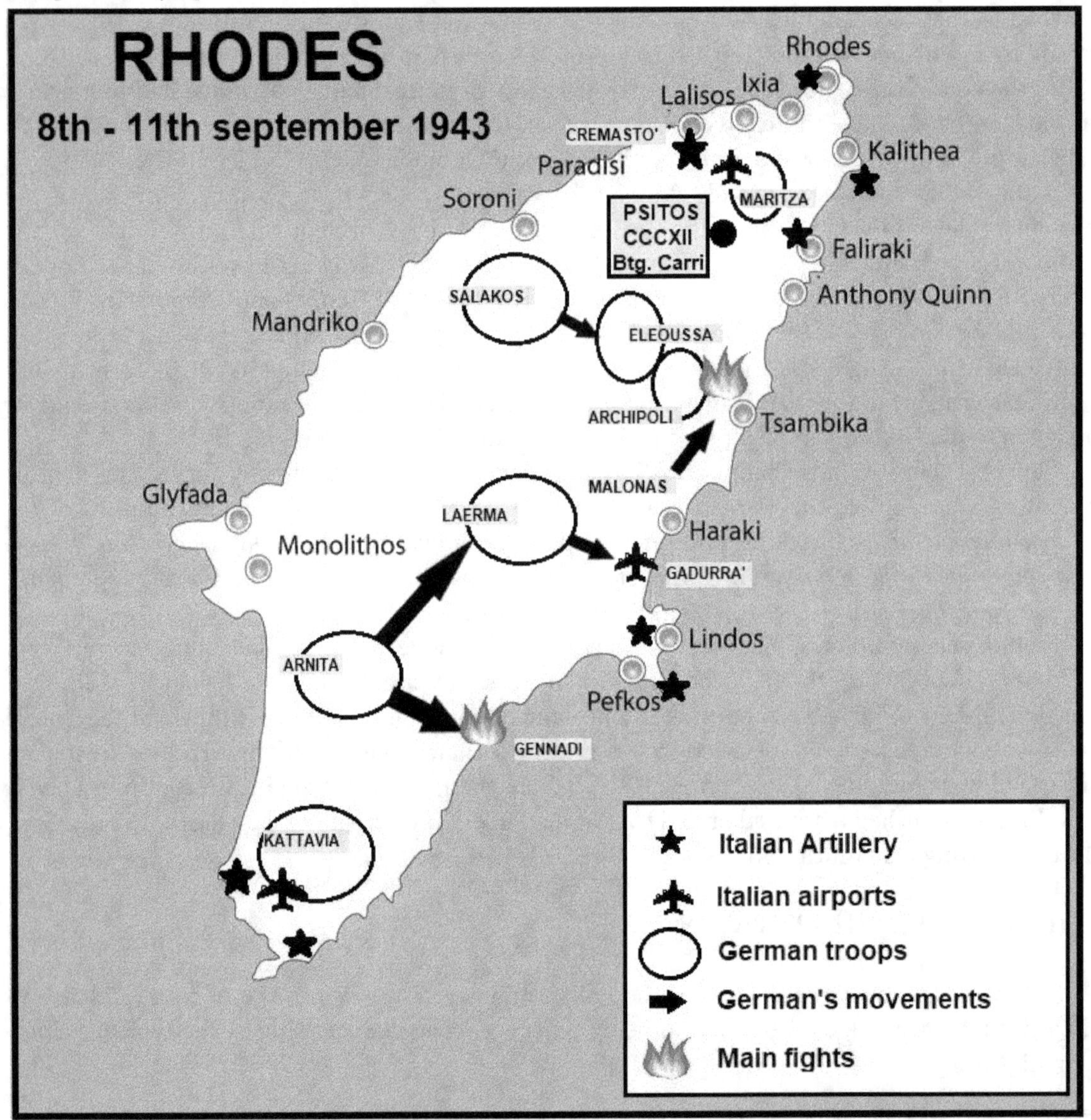

▲ Synthetic map of the clashes sustained in Rhodes between 8 and 11 September 1943, taken from the original preserved in the Military Historical Diary of the "Regina" Division.

The last change in the department took place in the middle of June 1943, when the Aegean Armored Car Bersaglieri Platoon arrived from Italy. This unit was set up on 1 September 1942 to be assigned, with a theoretical allocation of 4 AB41 armored cars, to the future "Giovani Fascisti" Armored Division; hijacked to Rhodes on 13 June 1943, the Platoon instead received the old Lancia 1ZMs, of which, in all probability, only 2 remained in perfect operational efficiency.

The Armistice also arrived unexpectedly in the Dodecanese and the troops deployed there, having received contradictory orders, reacted differently.

On the evening of 8 September 1943, approximately 37,500 Italian soldiers were present in Rhodes, according to data from the Italian General Staff; the German armed forces numbered about 7,500 men: a few months earlier Hitler had ordered the formation of the Sturmdivision "Rhodos" (also equipped with efficient armored units with 25 Panzer IVs, 15 self-propelled Stugs and about 150 armored vehicles of various kinds, against which the scarce Italian armored forces of the CCCXII Battalion could have done very little)[13] with the aim of maintaining its important position in the eastern Mediterranean even in the event of an allied landing in Italy and the consequent capitulation of the Savoy monarchy.

Even the Aegean troops were caught unprepared by the announcement of the Armistice: the memorandum of the Supreme Command for the Forces in the Aegean for the command on the spot (EGEOMIL), which should have been transmitted to the island by air, was not yet been delivered. The messenger, who was supposed to take him by air to Rhodes, was still stuck in Pescara on 9 September due to bad weather.

The lack of information and the few orders received forced the governor of the Dodecanese Inigo Campioni to make difficult choices. While the Wehrmacht asked him to cooperate, hoping for British aid that never actually arrived, Admiral Campioni decided to resist the Germans. In the meantime, the Germans took control of the road junctions and moved to the two airports, occupying them. Campioni then tried to negotiate General Ulrich Kleemann, commander of the German forces in Rhodes, simultaneously ordering the Italian troops to "resist without firing", but, frustrated by the situation, some units began to fight, forcing the Germans to surrender.

The Companies of the CCCXII Tank Battalion were located in what was identified as the "Piazza di Rodi Sector", near the main city of the island, in a static defense position, without specific movement orders in case of attack, while in Psito an aliquot of wagons had been retained, with the function of mobile reserve, to be used possibly to respond to any infiltrations in the Villanova area, a reserve made up of a Platoon of 4 L3 wagons.

The CCCXII, however, did not take part in clashes against the Germans, but handed over their arms. On 9 September the crews of the Lancia armored cars set fire to their vehicles along the road to Rhodes, for fear that they would fall into German hands.

Despite the numerical superiority of the Italians (about 40,000 Italian soldiers against only 7,000 Germans) and despite the majority of the soldiers being ready to fight, on 11 September the governor ordered the surrender, while some Italian units still fired. During the clashes of 10 and 11 September the Italian losses amounted to 152 fallen and 214 wounded.

---

13 The SturmBrigade "Rhodos", also known as Sturm-Division "Rhodos" was formed in May 1943, after the collapse of the Heeresgruppe "Afrika" in North Africa. Composed of 7,500 men under the command of Generalleutnant Ulrich Kleemann, it was stationed on the island of Rhodes and had incorporated elements of the 22. Infanterie-Division already present on the island and minor units stationed in the Aegean islands (a Battalion of about 1,000 men was on the island of Karpathos). However, the Division's efficiency was not very high, because some of the soldiers who made it up were former political prisoners or common prisoners, who had been offered a chance to redeem themselves through conscription. After the surrender of Castelrosso, Kleemann attacked the Italian garrison on 9 September, forcing it to surrender on 11 September. On 17 October 1944 the Division was formally dissolved and a large part of it was incorporated into the Panzergrenadier-Division "Brandenburg". Rhodes and the Dodecanese islands thus passed under the control of the "Kommandant Ost-Ägäis", formed by the elements of the Sturm-Division and the other army units remaining on the island.

The CXIII Tank Battalion of the Aegean was dissolved on 11 September, after the surrender of all the Italian units to the German Square Command in Rhodes. Furious fighting instead took place between Italians and Germans on the island of Kos and especially in Leros, which, although reinforced by English troops, had to surrender to the Germanic armed forces (Kos on 4 October, Leros resisted until 16 November). At home, the Royal Aegean Army Mixed Depot had no better fate. The city of Barletta was occupied by German troops in the night between 8 and 9 September; the Depot was initially "spared", but in the following days, following a pre-established and well thought-out plan, the Depot was attacked by Germanic units and robbed of all goods (food, clothing, ammunition) stored inside. Campioni was interned by the Germans in the Schokken and Thorn camps in Posnania, then handed over to the authorities of the Social Republic, who sentenced him to death for treason and shot him in Parma on May 24, together with Admiral Mascherpa, defender of the island of Lero[14]. The remaining troops on the island of Rhodes were disarmed and taken prisoner. A part of them chose to collaborate with the German armed forces in the following days, being incorporated into the Whermacht or joining the R.S.l. (about 3,000 men).

Most of the Italian soldiers, however, refused to support the German cause and were consequently interned: there were about 32,000 prisoners in Rhodes, 3,000 in Kos and 7,600 in Leros. From 11 September to 31 December about 1,200 Italian soldiers managed to escape in the most disparate ways; many of them, including some tankers of the CCCXII, tried to escape to Turkey, either by swimming or by keeping afloat, and many were killed by the Germans, but some succeeded in the enterprise, miraculously saved. The Italian military internees, who were instead captured while fleeing, were sent to the transit camp of Calato and then transferred as "prisoners of war" to Greece. Some Italian soldiers, who escaped capture, managed to give life to isolated episodes of resistance, which however did not produce appreciable results.

Part of the military internees in Rhodes (at least 5,000 by the end of September 1943) were employed for heavy manual work, such as the rehabilitation of roads or the construction of defensive works or, even, forestry works, and framed in Workers Battalions (Bau Battalionen).

Most of the tankmen were taken prisoner and interned in concentration camps, which were located in different locations on the island (altogether 42,000 Italian soldiers were imprisoned in the entire archipelago). The Germans organized 8 main prison camps for the Italian military in Rhodes:
- Camp number 1 = Rodi
- Camp number 2 = Asguro
- Camp number 3 = Afando
- Camp number 4 = Damatrià
- Camp number 5 = Campochiaro
- Camp number 6 = Calato
- Camp number 7 = Vati
- Camp number 8 = Apollacchia

Subsidiary camps depended on each camp, often located in locations functional to the employment of inmates in forced labor activities. Given the difficulty in providing for the needs of such a large number of prisoners of war, some of them were evacuated by ship, but many of them lost their lives due to the sinking of the ship; to obviate the impossibility of transport by sea, about half of the prisoners were transported to Germany by JU52 transport aircraft.

We remember the main tragedies of the sea that struck Italian internees during their travels to detention in Germany. On 23 September 1943 the "Donizetti" was torpedoed by British destroyers, killing 1,825 men, and on 8 February 1944 the steamship "Petrella" was torpedoed, and 2,646 of the 3,173 Italian prisoners on board died.

---

14 Both were awarded the Medal of Military Valor in memory by the Italian State.

The most terrible tragedy was that of the Norwegian steamship "Oria", a 2000-ton ship, launched in 1920, requisitioned by the Germans. The "Oria" set sail on 11 February 1944 from Rhodes at 5.40 pm headed for Piraeus, carrying 4,046 Italian prisoners on board (43 officers, 118 non-commissioned officers, 3885 soldiers, who had refused to join the RSI or collaborate with the Germans), 90 German soldiers on guard or passing through and the Norwegian crew. The following day, February 12, caught by a storm, the steamship sank near Cape Sounion, 25 miles from its final destination, after being stranded in the shallow waters overlooking the island of Patroklou. The rescues, hampered by the bad weather conditions and arrived only the following day, managed to save only 37 Italians, 6 Germans, 1 Greek, 5 crewmen. All the other occupants of the ship lost their lives, among them many tankers of the CCCXIII Mixed Aegean Battalion.

During the two years of German occupation about 200 Italians were shot and 150 inmates died of malnutrition. Life in the camps was in fact extremely hard and food and hygiene conditions precarious: food shortages were a constant for Italian prisoners and diseases such as scabies and cholera were widespread.

In October 1944 the Germans evacuated the Aegean. 6,356 Germans and 4,097 Italians remained in Rhodes, transformed into a military stronghold. There is no data on the number of internees in this group that remained in Rhodes until May 1945: only the end of the war put an end to the imprisonment of these Italian soldiers..

JOINING R.S.I.

Even in this remote corner of the Aegean, however, the Armistice had divided consciences: a part of the tank crews of the CCXII Battalion asked and obtained permission to continue hostilities alongside those they still considered allies, namely the Germans, by joining the Italian Social Republic.

1st Rhodes Tank Platoon

In Rhodes, after the Armistice, the figure of Major Carlo Migliavacca, an infantry officer, stood out, who worked to persuade the Italian military, pushing them to join the Italian Social Republic and enlist in the Republican armed forces or German[15]. After gathering a certain number of volunteers, on October 17, 1943 a ceremony was held for the rearmament of the Italian military in Campochiaro, which was attended by Migliavacca himself.

With the tanks present on the island of Rhodes, presumably no more than a dozen, the 1st Tank Platoon was formed, with a staff of 1 officer and 135 non-commissioned officers and troops. The Platoon was attached to the "Italian Regiment of Rhodes" ("Italienisch Rhodos Regiment")[16], framed in the Sturmdivision Rhodos. The Regiment was mainly made up of the Blackshirt departments of the "Regina" Division, joined by the legionaries of the National Security Militia, located in the Sporades and Cyclades islands, and about 1,900 soldiers of the dissolved Royal Army.

As of December 31, 1944, the force of the Platoon consisted of 1 officer and 55 non-commissioned officers and troops.

---

15 Joining the armed forces could take place as "Kampfwillige" or "KaWi" (volunteers in the German army) or "Hilfswillige" or "HiWi" (volunteer auxiliaries) and in both groups the Führer had to be sworn in. Initially, Migliavacca's work in Rhodes achieved limited success and only 10 officers and 180 non-commissioned officers and troops presented themselves as KiWi and as HiWi 45 officers and 1,859 non-commissioned officers and troops.

16 In other documents the department is referred to as the "Rhodes Volunteer Regiment". The Regiment was established in June 1944 with the various departments formed in the previous months with the Italians who had offered themselves as KaWi or Hiwi: 3 Blackshirt Battalions, 3 Constructors Regiments, the Tank Company, a Communications Company and a Health Company. Commander of the Regiment was the Lieutenant Colonel Cerullo., Nominated "Inspekteur der italienische Verbaende Ost-Ägäis".

According to a report by the Army General Staff dated 5 August 1944[17], the "1st Plot. Carri "L" already in the Aegean "resulted in Germany in Bergen, at the local Panzertruppenschule. In fact, from cross-analysis with other documents, it is clear that in Bergen at that time there were only 4 tank officers, coming from the 1st tank depot of Verona, and therefore the platoon was never transferred to Germany. In fact, the same table drawn up on 1 March 1945, the 1st Platoon L Chariots is indicated as present in the Aegean.

Probably not all the tanks of the dissolved CCCXII Mixed Tank Battalion present in Rhodes at the date of the Armistice were reused by the 1st Tank Platoon: according to some documents in November 1943 the Leichter Pz.Aufkl.Zug was created, which had to use means Italians of war prey. The unit, included in the Panzer Abteilung "Rhodos", had at that date 3 CV35 light tanks and 3 unidentified armored vehicles, indicated as "M304", which in February 1944 had risen to 4 and 3 means. The Leichter Pz.Aufkl.Zug then disappeared from the battle order in June 1944, it is not known whether because dissolved or assigned to another unit (it is possible that the tanks were actually absorbed by the 1st Italian Tank Platoon, later to the constitution of the Italian Regiment of Rhodes). The Regiment did not take part in firefights due to lack of enemies, mainly carried out police duties and surrendered, with the German garrison of the island of Rhodes, on 5 May 1945 to the Allies, after a demobilization ceremony held in the late afternoon.

51st Tank Platoon

In Crete, similarly to what happened in Rhodes, at the time of the Armistice, the "Siena" Division, presiding over the island, dissolved in Crete after 8 September as a result of the events; present were the L3 tanks of the 51st L Carri Company, which remained on the island after the "Merkur" operation. While the Germans were preparing to occupy the entire island, the CLXI Battalion "M" Black Shirts of Assault, deployed there together with the "Siena" Division and personnel of the Royal Navy, immediately sided with the Germanic armed forces, together with the coastal battery personnel. Thus was formed the "Italian Legion of Volunteers Crete", under the command of Lieutenant Colonel Gianoli.

Thanks to the influx of personnel from the "Siena" Division, which wished to continue fighting with the Germans, and to the work of recovering military material abandoned by the dissolved Division, the CLXI "M" Battalion was able to remain autonomous and was able to set up a department tank (51st Tank Platoon), which was deployed to Rethymno, with a force of 22 men. The Battalion, which was formally part of the Republican National Guard, faced some enemy attacks coming from the sea and, above all, from the air, also suffering from the inconveniences related to isolation and scarcity of food.

The Legion "Italian Volunteers Crete" laid down their arms on May 4, 1945, together with the German units. For the Italian soldiers loyal to the Social Republic, who were in the Dodecanese, this opened a long period of imprisonment in Kenya.

FALLEN OF THE BATTALION

As we have seen, the CCCXII was located in an area far from the war clashes and the main fronts and was not involved in any war action, with the exception of the occupation of the island of Crete. He therefore did not have to complain of war losses (not even during the "Merkur" operation) and the only two fallen in the Battalion, whose names are listed below, were caused by accidents:
- Tanker Benevento Gaetano, died October 31, 1941;
- Tabker Cavallo Francesco, died March 8, 1942.

---

17 "Reparti autonomi dislocati fuori dal teatro operativo italiano".

It is also known the name of a tanker, who died at the end of the war, as a result of the sufferings suffered in captivity:

- Tanker Gattulli Giuseppe, died in June 1945.

Most of the fallen of the Battalion are instead attributable to the terrible imprisonment, both in the Aegean and in Germany, and to the tragic sinking at sea of the ships that transported thousands of Italian internees, destined from the Aegean to Germany and which were sunk. In particular, we remember the numerous dead and missing from the sinking of the aforementioned steamship "Oria", on board of which there were many tank crews. Reconstructing all their names is hard work (also because the Germans did not compile any boarding lists and therefore most of them remain unknown), we mention in these few lines some names such as that of Corporal Giuseppe Fiorucci, Lieutenant Augusto Durgante Augusto, of the tanker Cosimo Barbato, of the tanker Pasquale Iengo or of the tanker Giuseppe Forcina, all perished in the fateful night between 11 and 12 February 1944.

▲ Anti-aircraft battery stationed above the walls of the walled city of Rhodes (ACS).

▲ An image of the deck of the "Porto di Roma" ship underway: in the foreground the casemate of a L3 wagon (Tallillo) is seen.

▲ The ship "Porto di Roma" ready to leave the port of Rhodes, overloaded with armored vehicles, motor vehicles, tank crews, Carabinieri and Black Shirts. The number of the "CCCXII" Battalion (Arena) stands out on the casemate of the L3 wagons.

▼ L3 tanks and FIAT 508CM Colonial cars on the deck of the "Port of Rome" sailing towards Crete (Arena).

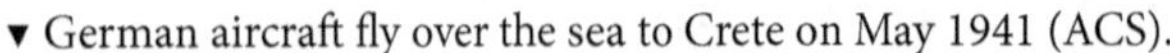

▲ Infantrymen of the "Regina" Division leaving for Crete (private collection).

▼ German aircraft fly over the sea to Crete on May 1941 (ACS).

▲ Some smiling tank crews of the CCCXI Battalion sing while sailing to Crete: many Italian soldiers took part in the operation with an almost goliardic spirit, as also told by some veterans, lacking awareness of the potential danger of the mission (private collection).

▲ A group of German paratroopers advances along a roadway in Crete: the German air-launch operation did not reach its planned objectives and risked turning into a defeat (private collection).

▼ Sailors from a landing department lead one of the small boats that were used during the landing in Sitia, to shuttle between the boats, where the Italian soldiers were, and the beach (ACS).

▲ Infantrymen of the "Regina" Division advance protected by a L3 / 33 (Tallillo) chariot.

▼ Land departments of the Regia Marina (ACS) also took part in the Italian landing.

▲ Italian infantry soldiers cautiously advance among the underbrush towards a position held by Greek soldiers (private collection).

▼ Positions on the Cretan coast near the landing point held by men of the navy and the Army (private collection).

▲ Italian advanced command post equipped with radio, organized by Italian soldiers in a small town of Crete (ACS).

▼ The L3 tanks of the CCCXII Battalion acted as vanguard of the Italian troops for the entire duration of the operations in Crete (Tallillo).

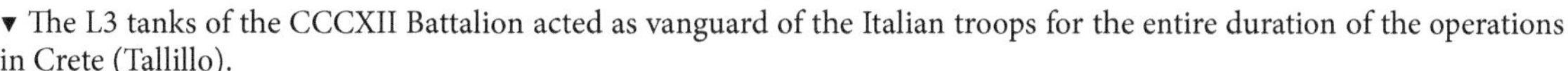

▲ Effects of the Italo-German attacks: British planes on fire in a Cretan airfield (ACS).

▼ German soldiers crawl as the British occupied sector in Crete is bombed on 28 May 1941 (ACS).

▲ A 47/32 anti-tank gun put on battery during the fighting (ACS).

▼ The crew of an L3 tank rests in the shade of an olive tree during a break (Welcome - Colonna).

▲ Some Italian tankers encounter a German tank at the crossroads of Jerapetra, target of the Italian Expeditionary Force, on May 30, 1941 (ACS).

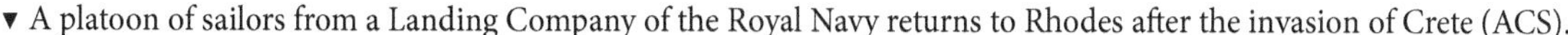

▲ Greek prisoners, photographed at the end of the fighting in Crete (ACS).

▼ A platoon of sailors from a Landing Company of the Royal Navy returns to Rhodes after the invasion of Crete (ACS).

▲ A group of Blackshirts in Crete awaits the visit of the Governor, in the spring of 1941, after the invasion of the island (ACS).

▼ General Ettore Bastico, Governor of the Italian Islands in the Aegean, reviews the Italian occupation troops in Crete, after the "Merkur" (ACS) operation.

▲ Vehicles of the Aegean Mixed Auto Department at Gadurrà airport in the winter of 1942: in the center you can recognize a CL39 light truck and, at the far right, a SPA 38R (ACS).

▼ Identification card of an Autiere of the 50th Aegean Mixed Auto Department. The department supplied the CCCXII Mixed Tank Battalion with the heavy trucks needed to move armored vehicles on the island of Rhodes (private collection).

▲ A German soldier inspects the 1ZM armored cars abandoned (and probably set on fire) by the crews of the Armored Car Platoon on the road to Rhodes on 9 September 1943.

▼ The same armored cars robbed of tires: you can recognize the rear "RE 88B" of the car in the foreground.

▲ Tanks of the Sturmdivision "Rhodos" marching along the walls of the port of Rhodes after the Armistice.

▼ A Panzer IV Ausf.G of the Sturmdivision "Rhodos" penetrated the interior of the old city of Rhodes after the events following 8 September.

▲ Regia Aeronautica CR-42 biplanes in an airport in the Dodecanese (Arena).

▼ A ground department of the Royal Navy Naval Base of Lero photographed a few days before September 8 (Arena).

▲ A German soldier in Leros scans the horizon, during the bloody clashes that took place on the island following the Armistice (Arena).

▼ Italian officers confer with German soldiers in Rhodes at the end of the clashes following the Armistice (Pisanò).

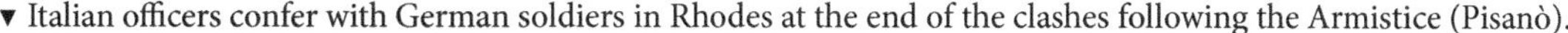

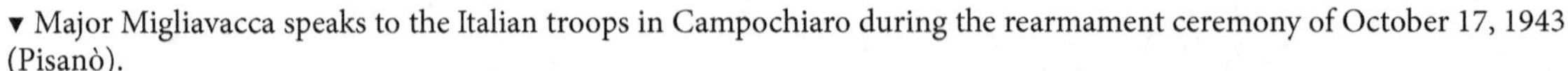

▲ About 8,000 Italian soldiers joined the Italian Social Republic in the Dodecanese. Fundamental was the work of Major Migliavacca who tirelessly toured Rhodes and the nearby islands to plead the cause of fascist Italy, convincing hundreds of soldiers of the dissolved royal troops to support the German armed forces (Pisanò).

▼ Major Migliavacca speaks to the Italian troops in Campochiaro during the rearmament ceremony of October 17, 1943 (Pisanò).

▲ In Campochiaro (Rhodes) on 17 October 1943 a ceremony was held to rearm the first Italian units in the Aegean which had joined the R.S.I. (Pisanò).

▲ Tanker Luigi Russo, a soldier of the CCCXII Mixed Tank Battalion of the Aegean, who died in the tragic sinking of the steamship "Oria".

▲ The tankman Giuseppe Forcina, another victim of the shipwreck of the night between 11 and 12 February 1944 (Forcina family archive).

▲ The steamship "Oria", on board which more than 4,000 Italian prisoners died, in the night between 11 and 12 February 1944.

▼ May 1945 Italian prisoners who survived the harsh living conditions of the secondary detention camp "Casa dei Pini a Rodi", photographed by the English troops who landed on the island after the German surrender in May 1945.

TESTIMONIES

CORPORAL ANTONIO FRAGASSI

When Antonio Fragassi was asked in which department he had fought, he proudly replied: *"Fourth Tank Regiment, three hundred and twelve Autonomous Tank Battalion of the Aegean".* Mr. Antinio, born in 1920, was one of the veterans of this department and I was lucky enough to be able to interview him, through his nephew Alessandro, when he was still alive. Despite his no longer young age, he still remembered many details of "his" war on him in that remote corner of "the Empire". Here is his story.

"I was recalled to arms and destined for the Tankers, they sent me from Pescara to Rome to the 4ᵗʰ Regiment, where I stayed for about a month to carry out training. After this period they sent me to the island of Rhodes, I left on February 13 or 14, 1940. I reached the island of Rhodes where the 312ⁿᵈ Battalion was deployed and I remained there for the duration of the war, which was all there in the Dodecanese. all in all quiet. In Rhodes I was placed in the 3ʳᵈ Light Tank Company and I followed the course to pilot the L3 light tanks. The Battalion was also equipped with old FIAT 3000 tanks: when we piloted them we were forced to drive blindly, keeping the hyposcope closed due to too much dust entering from the slot, and the direction to be taken was indicated by the commander who beat with the feet on the shoulders, according to a pre-established code, which represented the different directions to take.

Until June 10, 1940 we lived as if we were on vacation; the relationships we had with the local population were rather lukewarm, even if at times some love was born with the local girls or some friendship between peers. I became familiar with an Orthodox priest and it seemed a rather bizarre thing that this priest had to marry before being able to celebrate religious services.

On Sundays it was customary for us to attend the Holy Mass in the camp, which was followed by a march and the cleaning of our armored vehicles. We often practiced skill exercises at the controls of our tanks, and what we did most frequently was to have the light tank right after it had been tipped onto a mound of earth with a jack, which was hanging from the rear of the hull. I was the fastest of the whole Company to carry out the righting and this earned me the promotion to corporal, after only three months that I had obtained the pilot license of light tanks.

The ration that was distributed to us was good, every day we received a ration of 5 cigarettes and a dose of quinine against malaria, the wages were £ 1 per day, which was raised to £ 5 with the outbreak of the war.

With the onset of the conflict, the situation changed and the tanks were deployed to various locations on the island of Rhodes; the wagons were placed on the territory in teams of 3 vehicles, in positions such as to provide protection against possible landings and to garrison the surrounding areas. Thanks to the rank of corporal that I had conquered, I was entrusted with the command of a team of 3 tanks; for fear of enemy bombing, the controls moved the sections of tanks every 3 months from one village to another.

Unfortunately, our tanks were not equipped with radios and the only one available was at the Command, a device that was also used by an artillery unit located on the heights of the island. When the need arose to communicate with superiors, one or two tankers were forced to walk to the Command to receive orders or transmit information.

I remember the visit that Mussolini made to the island of Rhodes at the beginning of the war, it was the first and only time that I had the opportunity to see this Duce up close, whom all of Italy spoke of.

When we had to do the mission on Crete, at first I too would have to participate, they also made us do an exercise a few days before. The evening before the departure we celebrated together with some comrades and we almost got drunk, as if we were leaving for a pleasure trip, but the next morning, arrived at the port with the tanks at the Afanto pier, the barge that was to be used to make us embark it had sunk to the bottom of the harbor and so we were cut off.

As the months went by, the fear of a possible British attack was getting stronger and many beaches were mined by a department of engineers; if the British had landed in my sector I would have given orders to my section of 3 tanks to open fire with all our (poor) tank weapons and I would not have succumbed to the last, although I perfectly understood that with my action I would have gotten very little result. The squads of tanks that garrisoned the island were moved more frequently, but this did not prevent the English enemies from often being able to hit the ammunition and fuel depots. We then discovered that a spy was hiding among our ranks, he was a naturalized Italian Greek, who was playing a double game and communicating with the enemy. He was caught red-handed by Militia soldiers while he was communicating with the British with a radio that he kept well hidden. They arrested him and after a trial he was publicly shot in front of us tankers and the local population. From that moment, as if by magic, the English were no longer able to strike with the same effectiveness.

Then came that ugly September 8, which created a lot of turmoil. We no longer knew what we had to do, we hoped to return home soon, there were some who rebelled against the Germans and resisted. But then what seemed like an opportunity to see our homes again turned into a long imprisonment, for those like me who had decided not to collaborate with the Germans and the Republic of Mussolini.

Until the Armistice I had not had any contact with the famous "German comrades" as they said in the bulletins and at that point I would have preferred not to see even one in those sad days and instead I happened to meet the first ones in those bad moments. My imprisonment in the hands of the Germans began on September 14, 1943, until February 9 of the following year I was interned in a camp in Rhodes. In order not to forget that bad period, I took note of all the prison camps that he visits on the island of Rhodes. I was then moved to Psitos until February 16th and then to Campochiaro, in the 5th Collection Camp, where I stayed until the 27th, when they moved me back to Arcipoli. On April 4 they took me to Villanuova, then on May 4 to Cremastò, but on the 15th I was hospitalized at the Campo di Rodi Hospital, because I had caught scabies. On the 24th they sent me back to Cremastò and I remained there until July 24th, when they made me return to Villanova. Many of these displacements were due to the fact that we moved to various prison camps according to the jobs we were assigned to. In fact, the Germans had framed us Italian prisoners who remained in the islands in wards of workers, because they needed manpower for the road works and for the fortifications; I was compulsorily "enlisted" in the II Bau Battaillon, in the 5th Compagnia Internati.

Thanks to this "enlistment" I saved my life a little. In fact, at a certain point, as we prisoners were too many for the Germans, they tried to send at least a part of the Italian internees to work in Germany, since they had a great deal of trouble providing food and accommodation for so many men. Thus naval convoys were sent, there was also an Italian officer who collected the names of those who volunteered to go there, a certain Lieutenant Giovanni D'Amico, who also proposed to me twice to go to Germany. I always refused, preferring the relative safety of a prisoner in Rhodes rather than facing an uncertain fate in Germany or who knows where in Europe. And in fact we received news that all the ships carrying the prisoners were torpedoed, with a large number of dead prisoners drowned and the Germans thus decided not to make more sea expeditions. I think Lieutenant D'Amico also had a bad end. In August he asked me for the last time if I wanted to leave, but by now I was enrolled in the Bau Battaillon and so it was impossible for me to be transferred, he practically took my place and so he died in the sinking of the ship "Oria".

On 8 August 1944 I was hospitalized again, this time at the 553rd Field Hospital for malaria, but after 11 days they deemed me fit to return to work in Villanova.

In addition to the hard work to which they forced us, the imprisonment was however very difficult due to the hygienic conditions, which often favored epidemics of scabies, but malaria was also very widespread. I took them both as I said earlier.

On September 27th I was moved to Bosco Reale, until November 24th and then to Arcipoli until December 7th, when I was transferred to Malona. On January 25, 1945, I had to be hospitalized urgently in the infirmary of the camp for a new attack of malaria and on February 4 they declared me able to work again. I remained in the camp of Malona until the war ended and the Germans surrendered, on April 28, 1945 the English arrived in Rhodes and we were all happy and happy, because we thought it was over. Instead we discovered for the second time that it was not yet time to go home. On the same 28 April I was captured by the English, who transported us to Salaco until 31 May. That day we embarked in the evening on the French ship "Ville d'Oran", headed for Italy. We landed in Taranto after 3 days, on 2 June 1945, but they still took us prisoners to the 42nd Campo Sant'Andrea. I stayed here for practically two months, until July 28, then they sent me to the Santa Teresa sorting camp until August 5. In the evening of that day I was finally free and I was able to catch a train to really go back to my house.

The first few days that I was back in Italy, however, I regretted Rhodes a little. The situation was very confused and the fate was uncertain. As a good farmer in Rhodes with my expert eye I had seen a lot of arable land and probably, with peace, I could have lived very well there too."

▲ Group photo of Corporal Antonio Fragassi with some fellow soldiers of the CCCXII Tank Battalion of the Aegean (Fragassi family archive).

▲ Corporal Antonio Fragassi in ordinary tank driver uniform (Fragassi family archive).

▲ Tank driver uniform, with the blue one-piece overalls, helmet and leather jacket (Fragassi family archive).

▲ In the summer period uniforms were worn for hot climates: note the insignia sewn on the collar of the shirt (Fragassi family archive).

▲ Corporal Fragassi aboard a motorcycle (Fragassi family archive).

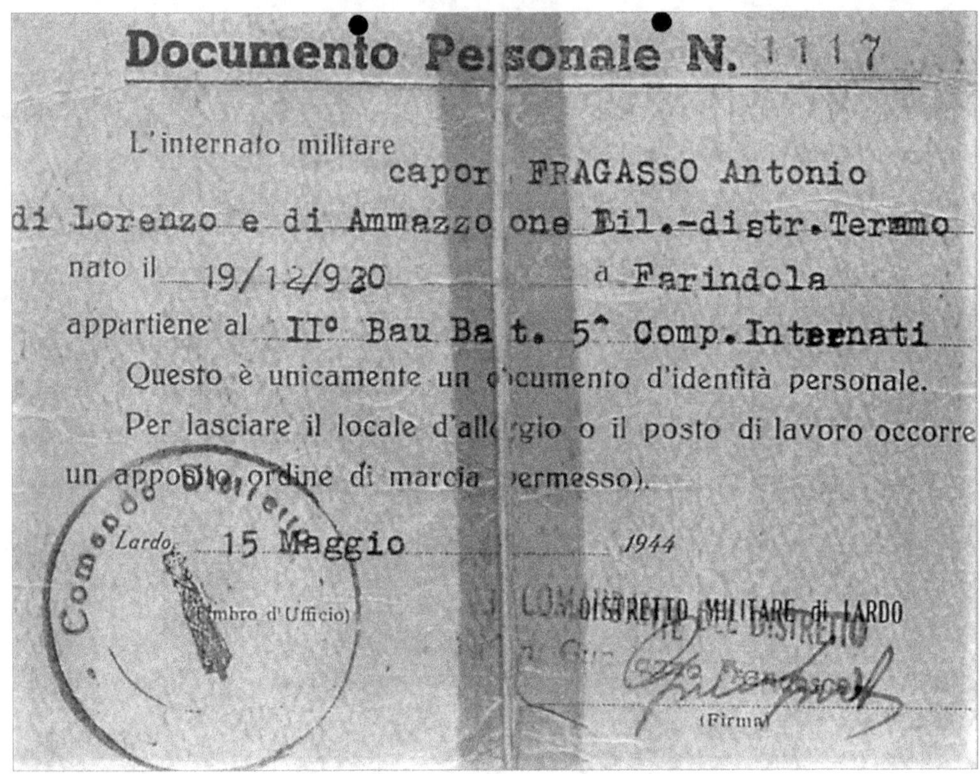

▲ Document dating back to the period of German imprisonment, which certifies the belonging of the inmate Antonio Fragassi to the II Bau Bataillon (Fragassi family archive).

▼ Identity card for prisoners of the Royal Army issued by the British authorities in Rhodes. It should be noted that in each document the surname of Antonio Fragassi has been distorted, depending on the nationality of the compiler (Fragassi family archive).

ATTESTA N° 380

che il militare Cpl. FRAGAZZI Antonio di Lorenzo

nato il 1920 distretto Teramo è rimasto internato dei tedeschi

dall'11 Settembre 1943 all'8 Maggio 1945

dal ======= al =====

in licenza dal ===== al =====

alla macchia dal ====== al =====

Rodi, li 31 Maggio 1945

IL PRESIDENTE

(Ing. Antonio Macchi)

Si afferma essere rispondente a verità quanto attestato dalla commissione.

Rodi, li 31 Maggio 1945

H.Q., 281 FORCE

▲ Certificate of prisoner of war status during the German occupation, drawn up by the competent military authorities and delivered to prisoners before embarking for Italy (Fragassi family archive).

▼ Antonio Fragassi's travel document, delivered to him on August 4, 1945, the day of his release from the allied prison camp of Taranto: from that moment he was once again a free man (Fragassi family archive).

Comando Campo "Tuker" Rimpatriati Italiani
TARANTO

DICHIARAZIONE

AL COMUNE di Farindola

Si dichiara che al Cap. Fragassi Antonio

è stata rilasciata da questo Centro una licenza di giorni sessanta + il viaggio a decorrere dal 4 AGO.

con scadenza

Si rilascia la presente per l'emissione della carta annonaria mod. M. I. P. (circ. 6155/S del 19-6-1944).

li

IL TEN. COLONNELLO COMANDANTE

Lieutenant Augusto Durgante

Lieutenant Augusto Durgante was assigned to the CCCXII Mixed Battalion of the Aegean, arriving in Rhodes at Psito, in August 1943, only a month before the tragic Armistice. After 8 September, Lieutenant Durgante was taken prisoner by the Germans and embarked on the steamship "Oria", on board which he perished in the tragic sinking of 11 February. This is the memory of him, in the words of his nephew Alberto:

"My uncle Augusto Durgante was born in Minerbe, in the province of Verona, on March 13, 1919 to Pietro Durgante and Eleonora Franco.

Enlisted as a non-commissioned officer in the 31ˢᵗ Tank Regiment, in the autumn of 1942 he participated in the 11ᵗʰ tank officer complement course in Florence, third tank regiment, obtaining various licenses, including the one for driving tanks. Until the end of July - early August 1943 he is in Rome at the 4ᵗʰ Tank Regiment, graduated as Second Lieutenant (with personal business card).

In August 1943 he was sent to the island of Rhodes and precisely in the town of Psito which is located in the center of the island, at the 312ⁿᵈ Tank Battalion with a military post address P.M. 550. Here it remains until 8 September 1943, the day of the armistice, which transforms my uncle and the tens of thousands of other Italian soldiers serving in the Greek islands into prisoners of war. The few letters received at the time came from the Feld Post Nummer (it is the postal code used by the Germans for the receipt and forwarding of mail from one of their prison camps in Greece) 0665K initially, subsequently by the FPN: 5418-2317 and in last from the FPN 03800C. From investigations into postal history all these F.P.N. they correspond to the secondary prison camp of Psito which is part of the main prison camp of Campochiaro (camp number 5 of the 7 present in Rhodes). The last letter was received in February 1944 and dated 9 February, a few days before the forced embarkation on the Oria ship and its sudden tragic sinking on 12 February 1944.

At the time, fruitless searches followed at Consulates, the International Red Cross, prison camps of the then Yugoslavia, research messages transmitted by radio, until 1957, the date of the latest research documents available. A further contact of the time (obviously at the time the information was very chaotic and sometimes unreliable or close to looting), stated that he had been embarked on this steamer but that he was saved and remained with him a prisoner in a German concentration camp in Yugoslavia (Zemun and / or Dubronvichi).

The only certain thing is that my uncle Augusto Durgante never returned home and my father Attilio (brother of Augusto) and his family, have long carried the wounds of this loss in their hearts, which also causes uncertainty. on his real fate.

Memories of him remain, some photos, some letters received in those stormy years, a suitcase containing his uniform and the Italian flag with the eagle of the Kingdom of Italy and little else, including his name inscribed on the war memorial. present in the main square of Minerbe (VR), his hometown".

This is the sad text of the last letter received by the family, before losing all traces of Augusto:
"February 8ᵗʰ, 1944.

Dear,
the days pass and I never receive mail from you, even this single comfort has failed me. I do not know for my part you continue to receive it, how much joy it would give me if you at least received news from me. If by chance a long time passes without you being able to receive my staff, don't worry about me. As I have already told you, I cannot complain about the life I lead and the health I enjoy, needless to tell you how much I hope for your good health and a possibly peaceful life.

My only hope is to see everything over soon and possibly return safe and sound as soon as possible between you. I always believe Brunetto at home, that he goes to school regularly, I hope to guess as well as about my behavior towards Uncle Bepi. Here with me I have several companions from Verona who remind me of my country and my dialect every day.

With the hope of receiving some of your lines, always remembering you so much. Have an infinity of long kisses and your hugs

Augusto".

▲ Second lieutenant Augusto Durgante at the time of enrollment in the tank crew (Durgante family archive).

▲ Durgante during the course for additional officer student at the 3rd Tank Regiment of Bologna (Durgante family archive).

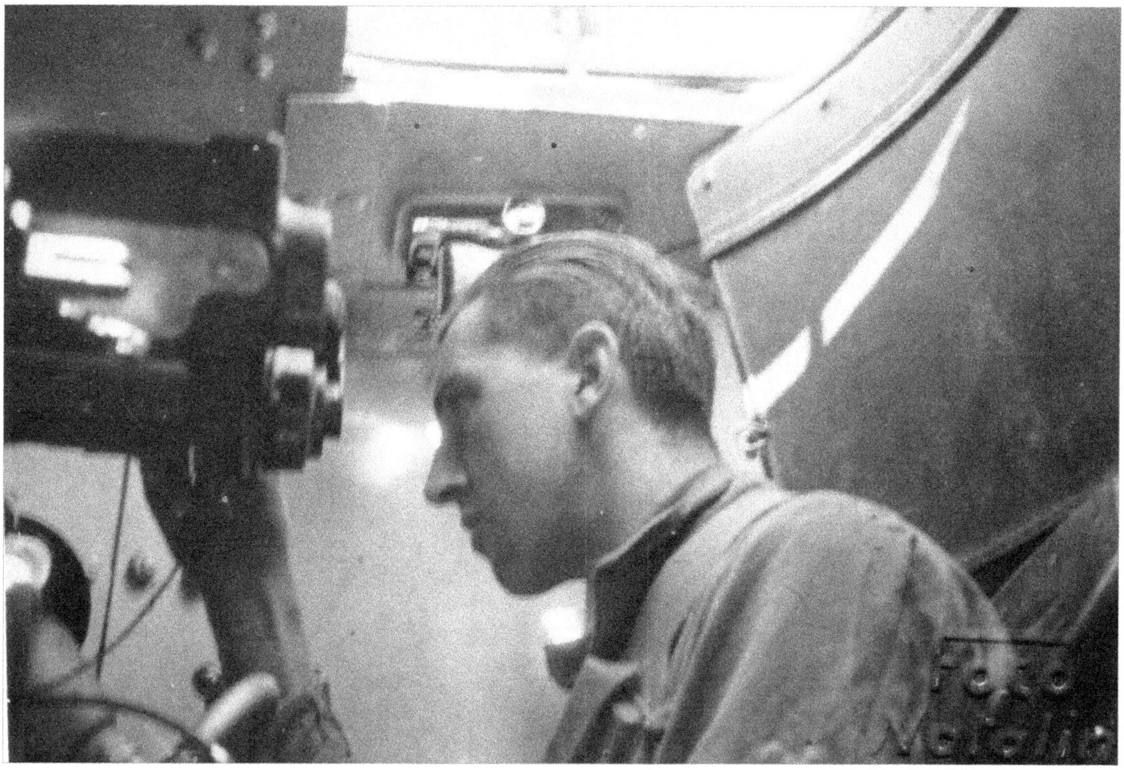

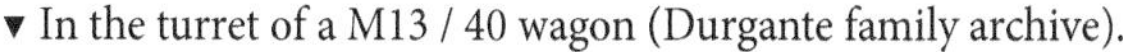

▲ Augusto Durgante inside the turret of an M chariot (Durgante family archive).

▼ In the turret of a M13 / 40 wagon (Durgante family archive).

▲ Durgante next to a medium tank M13 / 40, entirely painted in gray-green, probably the same as the previous images (Durgante family archive).

▲ During the Course for Additional Officer Cadets, the young tank crews were also trained in the driving of motorcycles, considered fundamental means to be used in the event of advance missions (Durgante family archive).

▼ Warlike portrait of the officer student Augusto Durgante aboard an L3 light tank (Durgante family archive).

▲ In the turret, with the protective leather jacket and helmet, used by the tankmen of the Royal Army (Durgante family archive).

▼ Augusto Durgante together with his fellow soldiers aboard a truck during the training (Durgante family archive).

▲ A L6 / 40 wagon in maneuver at the 3rd Tank Regiment of Bologna (Durgante family archive).

▼ An M wagon faces an obstacle on the test course of the 3rd Carristi (Durgante family archive).

REGIO ESERCITO ITALIANO

4° Reggimento **Carristi**

Btg. Addestramento

9ª Compagnia

RUOLINO MILITARE

tenuto dal

S.ten. Durgante Augusto

Presso Rinaldi - Via Lucca 33/4

Roma

▲ Military role of second lieutenant Augusto Durgante, held at the 4th Tank Regiment of Rome (Durgante family archive).

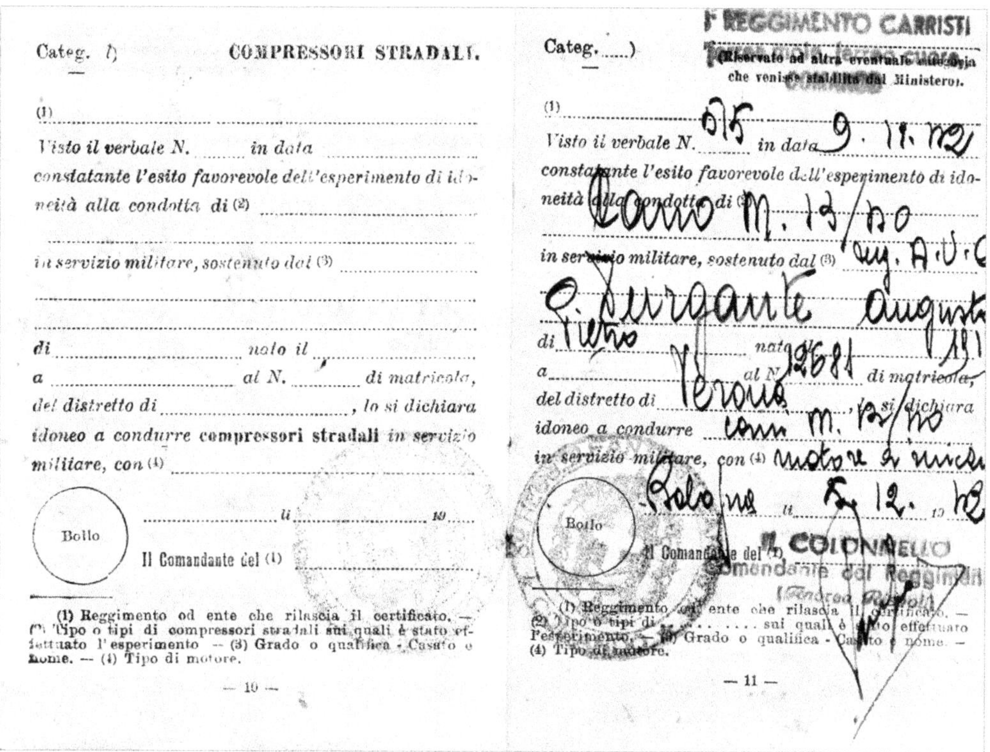

▲ Driving license for vehicles for military use, which also contains the certificate of qualification to drive M13 / 40 wagons, obtained by Augusto Durgante on 5 December 1942 at the 3rd Tank Regiment (Durgante family archive).

▼ Postcard of his father Pietro, sent to Augustus on 10 November 1943, and rejected by the German Armed Forces (Durgante family archive).

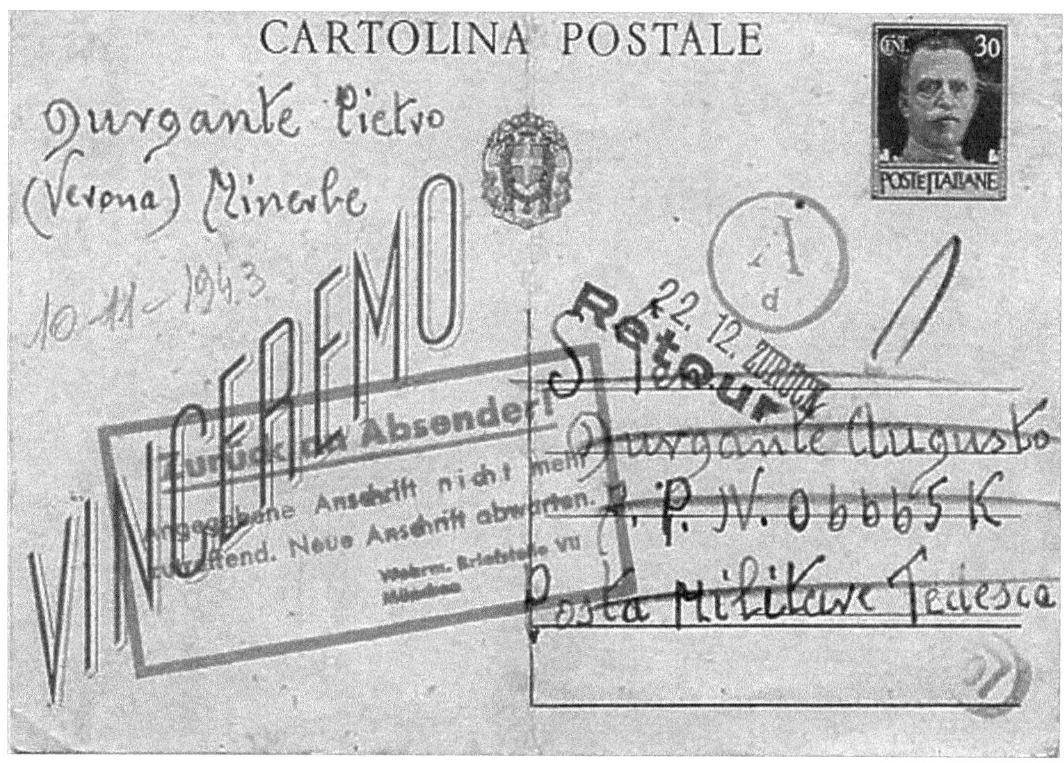

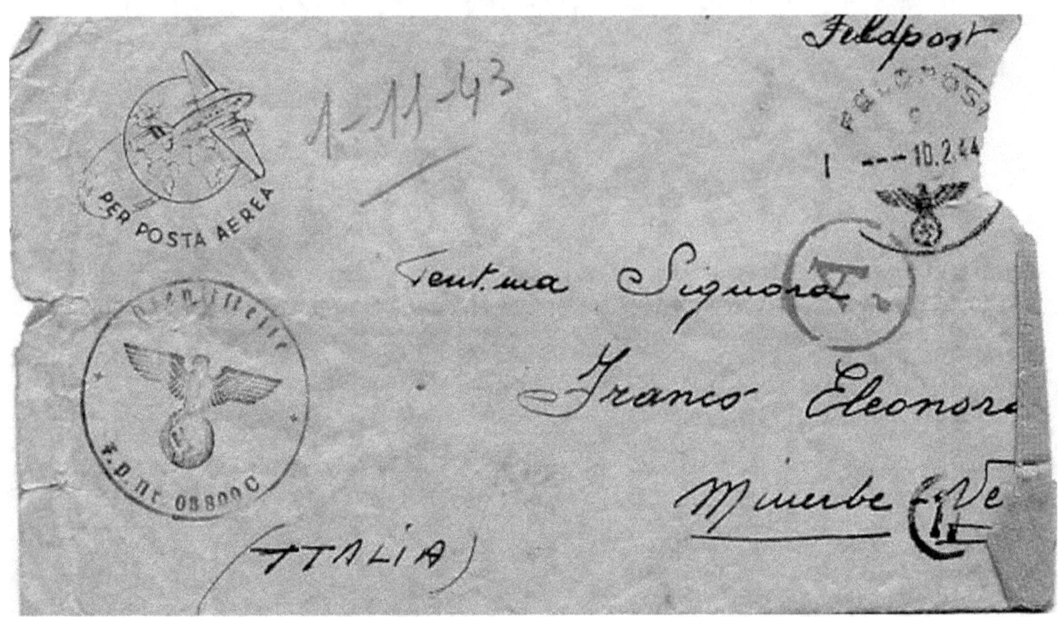

▲ Envelope of a letter sent by Durgante from captivity: bears the stamps of the Feldpost, identifiable with the secondary prison camp of Psito (Durgante family archive).

▼ The image of Augusto Durgante in uniform was also projected during the intermission of the "The Wall" tour, conducted between 2010 and 2013 by Roger Waters, leader of the famous Pink Floyd musical group. For Waters, war has always been an obsession, having suffered the trauma of the loss of his father during the landing of Anzio and many lyrics of his songs refer to the war and its tragic consequences. Roger Waters thus launched the "Fallen loved ones" initiative, with the aim of making the message of his show universal, that is, that sense of pain and loss that we all feel towards family members killed in a conflict, asking fans to send him the photos and a brief description of one's "fallen loved one", regardless of the front and the war fought. Durgante, passionate about the musical group, sent the photo of his uncle Augusto and so his face, together with that of all the others who had contributed to the project, appeared for several hundred evenings around cities all over the world and, subsequently, on the cover of one of the discs relating to the concert itself (Durgante family archive).

▼ In a touching series of images, we see the uniform of second lieutenant Augusto Durgante, kept by the family in a suitcase, together with a tricolor. The jacket, trousers, rigid cap and sachet have been preserved from the uniform. On these two there is the frieze as an officer of the 4th Tank Regiment, from which Durgante came before being sent to the CCCXII Tank Battalion in Rhodes; as we have seen, most of the tankmen stationed in Rhodes continued to have the number of the 4th Regiment of origin in the rod of the frieze (Durgante family archive).

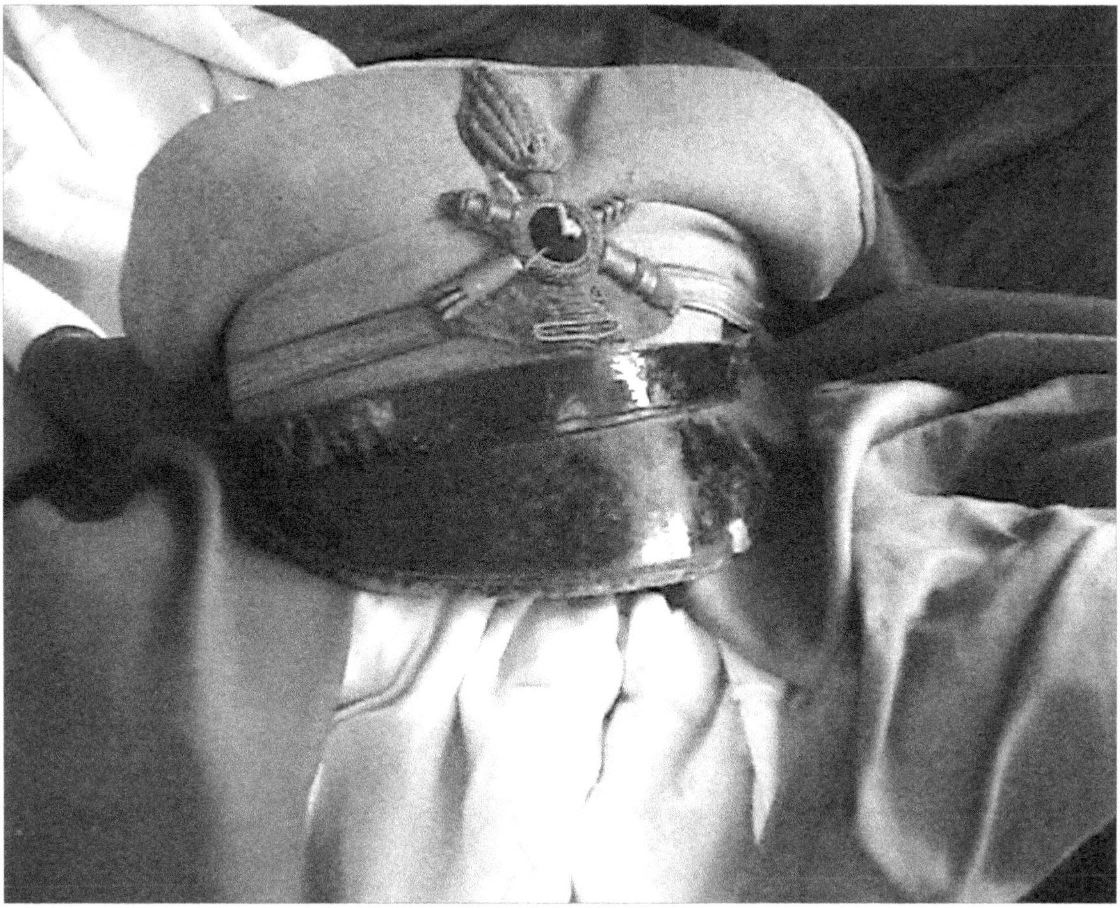

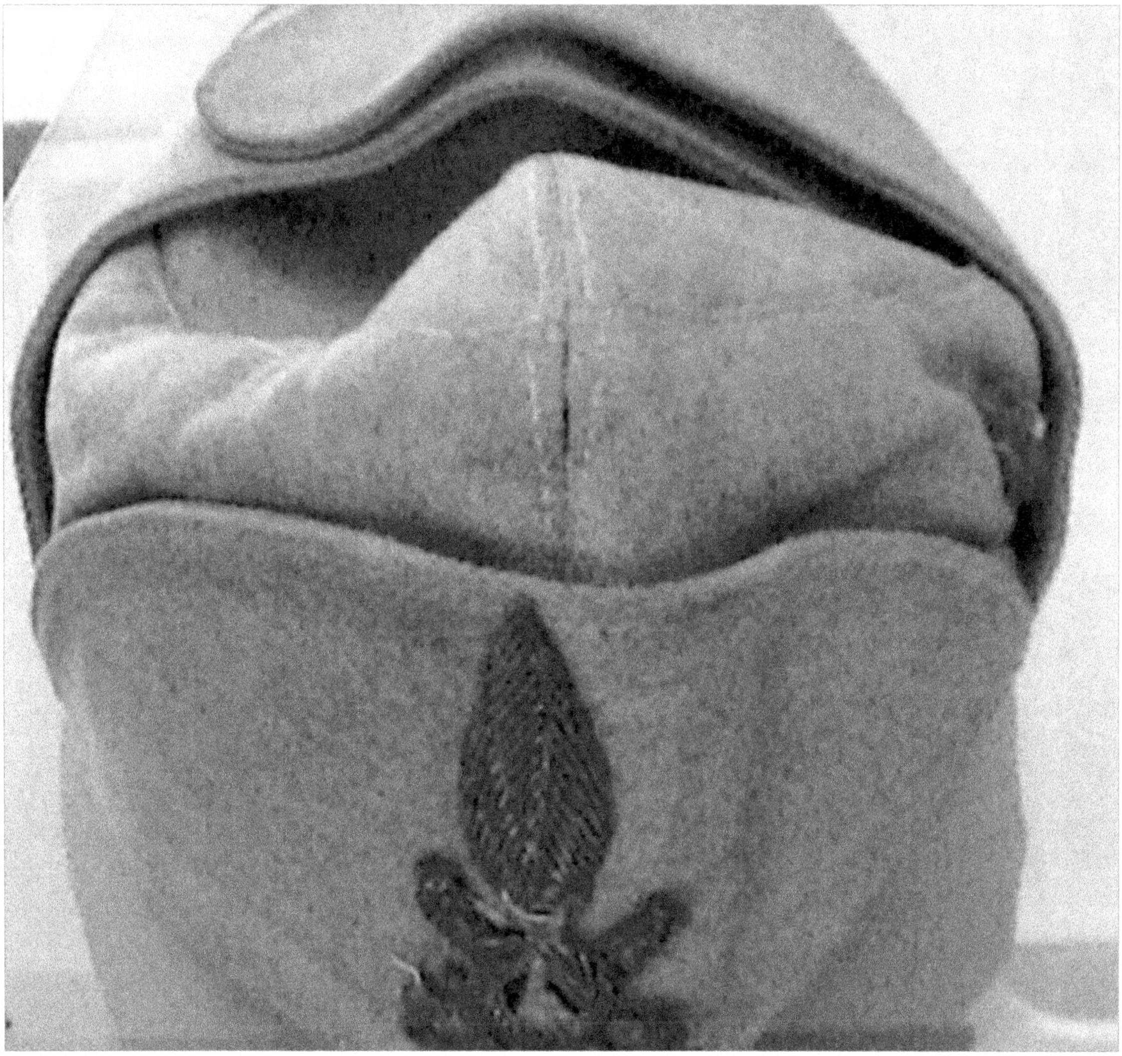

▲ The Medal of Honor for the internees of Augusto Durgante, delivered to the family on 2 June 2015. This honor is intended for all Italian citizens deported and interned in German concentration camps between 1943 and 1945, whether they are Italian military internees or civilians (Durgante family archive).

Tanker Pasquale Iengo

Pasquale Iengo was born in San Giorgio a Cremano (NA) on March 13, 1922. Called up to arms, he was assigned to the 312nd Tank Battalion of the Aegean and, after the Armistice, was taken prisoner by the Germans. Like many other soldiers in the unit, he was sent to internment in Germany and embarked on the steamship "Oria", where he perished with the other unfortunate Italian soldiers who were on board. Years later, Pasquale's sister received her brother's helmet and bayonet, which were found again by chance. At the time of the events, and for many years to follow, the family never managed to know Pasquale's fate; only many years later the brother, who with great determination had continued to search for news, with the scarce means available at the time, did he succeed in knowing that the relative could have died in the Aegean or in Libya. Only in 2021 the nephews, thanks to long searches done on the internet, were able to discover what happened to their uncle Pasquale in 1944 in Rhodes.

▲ A young tank driver Pasquale Iengo in Rhodes (Iengo family archive).

▲ Tanker Pasquale Iengo, who died in the sinking of the steamship "Oria" in the night between 11 and 12 August 1944, while he was being transported with 4,000 other Italian prisoners to mainland Greece (Iengo family archive).

▼ Group photo of Tankers of the CCCXII Tank and Infantry Battalion of the "Regina" Division. The infantrymen wear the gray cloth fatigue uniform of the Royal Army (Iengo family archive).

▲ Tanker Pasquale Iengo (standing second from right, with a mustache) with a fellow soldier (also wearing a gray-green uniform) in Rhodes (Iengo family archive).

Corporal Major Dante Pedonesi

And here is the memory of the tank driver Dante Pedonesi, of the 4th Tank Regiment, then transferred to the CCCXII Mixed Carri Battalion, in the story of his son Francesco:

"My father Dante, born in 1920, was born in the province of Fermo, then the province of Ascoli Piceno. He was a tanker of the 312nd Mixed Aegean Tank Battalion, extraction of the 4th Tank Regiment of Rome, he sailed from Bari to the Aegean on February 9, 1940. He was a corporal, belonged to the 1st Tank Company, then passed to the Command Company. He always told me that the department suffered a lot for the lack of fuel to run the "box" wagons. In 1941 he participated in Operation "Merkur" on Crete, with a few tanks, landing on the island when the games were over and there was no more fighting.

After the Armistice he managed to go into hiding and in 1944 he fled to Samos aboard a raft made with petrol drums; there he was captured by the English and taken prisoner to Suez, returning to Taranto on 20 July 1946.

After the war, he managed to get the body of one of his friends back to Italy from Rhodes, who had been shot by the Germans after 8 September, when they went into hiding. He had learned of the place where the Greeks had buried his friend and gave the information to his relatives: now he rests in Italy!".

▲ A rare image of a FIAT 3000 tank of the CCCXII Mixed Tank Battalion in operation in Rhodes (Pedonesi family archive).

▲ Tanker Dante Pedonesi of the CCCXII Mixed Tank Battalion of the Aegean with the uniform adopted on board the tanks (Pedonesi family archive).

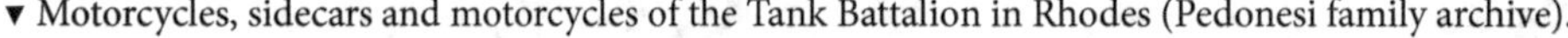

▲ Carristi of the CCCXII portrayed in a joking attitude, in the center the Pedonesi: in case of punishment, the Carristi's hair was cut to zero, as for the two soldiers portrayed in the photo with the bag sideways (Pedonesi family archive).

▼ Motorcycles, sidecars and motorcycles of the Tank Battalion in Rhodes (Pedonesi family archive).

▲ Group photo of the tankmen taken on Easter 1943 (Pedonesi family archive).

▼ The seat of the EGEOMIL Command in Rhodes (Pedonesi family archive).

▲ A more unique than rare photograph of one of the six armored cars launches 1ZM of the Armored Car Platoon of the CCCXII Carristi in Rhodes. The image clearly shows that, contrary to what has been believed up to now, these armored cars were painted exclusively in uniform gray-green (Pedonesi family archive).

▲ Group of Carristi of the CCCXII in a moment of relaxation (Pedonesi family archive).

▼ A group of tankmen on a carefree day by the sea. The photo is dated 5 September 1943, a few days before the huge tragedy of the Armistice (Pedonesi family archive).

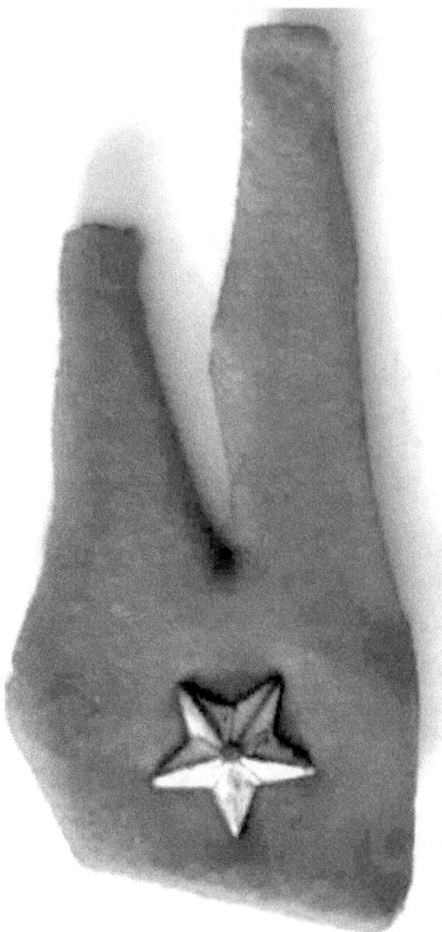

▲ What remains of the insignia of the Carrista Dante Pedonesi: unfortunately the blue under-tarnish was lost during his imprisonment and only the red flames were preserved (Pedonesi family archive).

▼ Cap of Dante Pedonesi, we note on the frieze the habit of keeping the number "4" identifying the Regiment of origin of the soldiers of the CCCXII Tank Battalion of the Aegean (Pedonesi family archive).

COLORING AND MARKINGS OF ARMORED VEHICLES

LANCIA 1ZM ARMORED CARS

Until recently, only two images of the Battalion's Lancia were known, taken after the cars were abandoned by the crews, following the surrender of the Italian troops. From these two photos it was assumed that the Lancias were painted in gray green, on which a mottled or lattice yellow camouflage had been applied.

In fact, a recent discovery shows more clearly that the armored cars had kept only the gray-green color and that what appeared to be a camouflage was nothing more than a thick layer of dust deposited on the bodywork, along the dirt roads of the island of Rhodes.

On the turret, on the sides and on the back, there were three rectangles, probably yellow, containing the number of the vehicle inside the Platoon, probably red. The Roman number of the CCCXII Battalion was written in white characters on the rear part of the busway sides.

The 6 armored cars of the Platoon were marked "RE 18B," RE 26 B "," RE 64B "," RE 68B "," RE 74B "and" RE 88B ".

Lancia 1ZM Plotone Autoblindo

FIAT 3000 TANKS

Unfortunately, the images depicting FIAT 3000 tanks of the Battalion are very scarce and of bad quality, so it was not possible to identify with absolute certainty the color of the vehicles, it is only possible to make hypotheses. Until 1939 the FIAT 3000 wagons adopted a livery entirely in reddish brown, which was gradually replaced during the scheduled maintenance with an entirely gray-green livery, therefore the wagons of the CCCXII could take on one of these two colors. It is also likely that the two colors coexisted within the department, since the gray-green color replaced the previous brown gradually and not in a single solution.

As far as the markings are concerned, the speech is simpler. The wagons of the CCCXII carried the red rectangle tactical markings in the turret (indicating the 1st Company): one on the back and two laterally in the center of the turret, as can be seen from the scant photographic documentation that has come down to us. This position was unusual, since on FIAT 3000 these two rectangles were usually placed on the front and not on the side. The Company Commander's chariot had a solid red rectangle, while the Platoons' chariots had one, two or three vertical white stripes, indicating the 1st, 2nd or 3rd Platoon respectively. For Platoon chariots, above the rectangular mark there was a white Arabic number, indicating the number of the chariot within the Platoon (the standard actually required that the chariot number must be of the Company's distinctive color).

In September 1940, a regulation was issued that sanctioned the adoption of the white Roman number identifying the Battalion on FIAT 3000 tankss on the central part of the turret, but this rule was largely disregarded. The CCCXII was the organic unit that complied with this requirement (the number was placed below the tactical rectangle), together with the CCCXXII Tank Battalion.

FIAT 3000 modello 21 (L5/21)

L3/33 AND L3/35 LIGHT TANKS

The CCCXII Aegean Tank Battalion had both L3 / 33 and L3 / 35 tanks. From the few images found it seems that the coloring of the wagons was not uniform: some appear with the pattern adopted on the fast wagons until the end of 1939, consisting of a camouflage with small black and dark green spots on a reddish brown background, others instead entirely painted in gray-green, livery that replaced the previous camouflage.

The rectangular tactical mark, placed on the sides of the superstructure, was blue for the 2nd Company and yellow for the 3rd Company. The Company Commander's chariot had a solid colored rectangle, while the Platoons' chariots had one, two or three vertical white stripes, indicating the 1st, 2nd or 3rd Platoon respectively. For the Platoon chariots, above the rectangular mark there was an Arabic number indicating the number of the chariot within the Platoon (from 1 to 4). By regulation, the wagon number had to be in the Company's distinctive color, but from the photos it is not clear whether this rule was respected or whether, as for the FIAT 3000 tanks of the same department, this number was white.

On the back of the casemate, on the left side at the top, was the Roman numeral indicating the Battalion in white letters.

BIBLIOGRAPHY

Books

- AA.VV., "Egeo italiano", Italia Editrice, Campobasso, 1994.
- AA.VV., "La storia fuori sacco", Città di Barletta, 2010.
- Arena Nino, "R.S.I. – Forze Armate della Repubblica Sociale – La guerra in Italia – 1943 – 1944 – 1945", Ermanno Albertelli Editore, Parma, 2002.
- Ascoli Massimo, "La Guardia alla Frontiera", S.M.E. – Ufficio Storico, Roma, 2003.
- Avagliano Mario, Marco Palmieri Marco, "I militari italiani nei lager nazisti. Una resistenza senz'armi (1943-1945)", Il Mulino, Bologna, 2021
- Baldi Gianni, "Dolce Egeo, guerra amara", Rizzoli, Milano, 1988.
- Benvenuti Bruno, Colonna Ugo, "Fronte Terra – L'armamento italiano nella Seconda Guerra Mondiale", volumi 1, 2/I e 2/II, Edizioni Bizzarri, Roma, 1972.
- Cappellano Filippo, Pignato Nicola, "Gli autoveicoli da combattimento dell'Esercito Italiano", volume I, S.M.E. – Ufficio Storico, Roma, 2002.
- Cappellano Filippo, Pignato Nicola, "Insegne, uniformi, distintivi e tradizioni delle Truppe Corazzate Italiane, T & T edizioni, 2005.
- Ceva Lucio, Curami Andrea, "La meccanizzazione dell'Esercito Italiano dalle origini al 1943", S.M.E. – Ufficio Storico, Roma, 1994.
- Corbatti Sergio, Nava Marco, "Come il diamante!", Laran Editions, Bruxelles 2008.
- Crippa Paolo "I reparti corazzati del Regio Esercito e l'Armistizio", Volume 2, Soldiershop Publishing, Zanica (BG), 2021.
- Crippa Paolo, "I Reparti Corazzati della Repubblica Sociale Italiana 1943 -1945", Marvia Edizioni, Voghera (PV), 2006.
- Crippa Paolo, "Italia 43 -45 - I mezzi corazzati italiani della Guerra Civile 43- 45", Mattioli 1885, Fidenza (PR), 2015.
- Cucut Carlo, "Le forze armate della RSI 1943-1945 – Forze di terra", Trento, Gruppo Modellistico Trentino di studio e ricerca storica, 2005
- Falessi Cesare, Pafi Benedetto, "Veicoli da Combattimento dell'Esercito italiano dal 1939 al 1945", Interama Books, 1976.
- Filippo Cappellano Filippo, Pignato Nicola, "Il Regio Esercito alla vigilia dell⌧8 Settembre 1943", Ermanno Albertelli Editore, Parma, 2003.
- Guglielmi Daniele, Tallillo Andrea, Tallillo Antonio, "Carro L3. Carri veloci, carri leggeri, derivati", GMT, Trento, 2004.
- Nino Arena Nino, R.S.I. Forze Armate della Repubblica Sociale – La guerra in Italia 1943, Parma, Ermanno Albertelli, 1999
- Parri Maurizio, "Tracce di cingolo – compendi generale di storia dei Carristi 1916 – 2016", A.N.C.I. Verona, 2016.
- Pasqualini Maria Gabriella, "L'esercito italiano nel Dodecaneso 1912-1943 – Speranze e realtà- I documenti dell'Ufficio Storico dello Stato Maggiore dell'Esercito", S.M.E. – Ufficio Storico, Roma, 2005.
- Pignataro Luca, "Il Dodecaneso Italiano 19142 – 1947", volume III "De Vecchi, guerra e dopoguerra",

- Pignato Nicola, "Dalla Libia al Libano 1921/1985", Editrice Scorpione, Taranto, 1989.
- Pignato Nicola, "Un secolo di autoblinde in Italia", Mattioli 1885, Parma, 2008.
- Pisanò Giorgio, "Gli ultimi in grigioverde", Edizioni F.P.E., Milano, 1994.
- Sandri Leonardo, "Reparti della R.S.I. nei Balcani ed in Grecia: settembre 1943 – maggio 1945", Edito in proprio, Milano 2021.
- Tallillo Andrea, Tallillo Antonio, "Carro FIAT 3000", GMT, Trento, 2018.
- Tallillo Andrea, Tallillo Antonio, "L'autoblindo Lancia 1Z. E le altre italiane del 1912-1945 (FIAT Arsenale, Isotta Fraschini, Bianchi e FIAT Terni)", GMT, Trento, 2021.
- Ufficio Storico dello S.M.E., "Le operazioni delle unità Italiane nel Settembre – Ottobre 1943" S.M.E. – Ufficio Storico, Roma, 1975

Articles

- Cocchia Aldo, "Aspetti navali dello sbarco italiano a Creta", in "Rivista Marittima", August - September 1951.
- Crippa Paolo, "Blindati italiani nel Dodecaneso" in "Milites", number 25, September - October 2007.
- Crippa Paolo, "Unità Corazzate nel Dodecaneso dopo l'Armistizio ", in "Ritterkreuz", numero 40 - anno 7, luglio 2015.
- Luciano Alberghini Maltoni Luciano, "Rodi 1943 – L'anno decisivo per le sorti del Dodecaneso", Storia Militare", numero 103, aprile 2002.
- Mattiello G., "I prigionieri italiani a Rodi dopo l'8.9.43", in "Notiziario AICPM", numero 57, febbraio 1990.
- Mondini Lorenzo, "L'Operazione "Merkur" e la Divisione Regina", in Storia Militare, numero 24, settembre 1995.
- Scalpelli Adolfo, "La formazione delle forze armate di Salò attraverso i documenti dello Stato maggiore della RSI", in "Il movimento di liberazione in Italia" numeri 72 e 73, a cura dell'I.N.S.M.L.I., senza editore, 1963.
- Schierano Mario, "Situazione delle truppe italiane nell'isola di Creta dopo l'8 settembre 1943", in "Studi Storico Militari", 1988 .
- Shenck Peter, "Dodecaneso 1943 – 1945", in "Storia Militare", numero 90, marzo 2001.
- Tocci Patrizio, "Le Autoblindo Lancia 1ZM", parte 2ª, in "Storia Militare", numero 68, maggio 1999.
- Tocci Patrizio, "Le Compagnie Carriste di Frontiera", in "Storia Militare", numero 84, settembre 2000.

Archivi

- Archivio famiglia Durgante
- Archivio famiglia Fragassi
- Archivio famiglia Iengo
- Archivio famiglia Pedonesi

TITOLI GIÀ PUBBLICATI - TITLES ALREADY PUBLISHING

SOLDIERSHOP
PUBLISHING
BOOKS TO COLLECT